CLASSICAL BUDO

CLASSICAL BUDO

THE MARTIAL ARTS
AND WAYS OF JAPAN

DONN F. DRAEGER

WEATHERHILL
BOSTON & LONDON

Weatherhill
An imprint of Shambhala Publications, Inc.
Horticultural Hall
300 Massachusetts Avenue
Boston, Massachusetts 02115
www.shambhala.com

Title page: Detail from a woodblock print by Sakuragawa Horimasa.

Text decorations and illustrations: Calligraphy by Kaminoda Tsunemori;
woodcuts from *Hokusai Manga Roku-hen*; a woodblock print sketchbook by
Gekkotei Bokusen, a disciple of Hokusai; *Kinsei Kyogiden* (A Modern Tale of
Chivalry), illustrated by Kaisai Honen (Yoshitoshi), published in 1918; *Sumo
Zushiki, Omote Yonju-hatte* (Figures of the Forty-eight Surface Techniques of
Sumo), vol. 4, published in 1930; and E. Papinot's *Historical and Geographical
Dictionary of Japan*, published in 1910. All photographs, except where credit
is given, are by the author.

First edition, 1973
First paperback edition, 1990
Fourth printing, 2007

Printed in the United States of America

♾ This edition is printed on acid-free paper that meets the American
National Standards Institute Z39.48 Standard.
Distributed in the United States by Random House, Inc.,
and in Canada by Random House of Canada Ltd

The Library of Congress Cataloging in Publication Data:
Draeger, Donn F. / Classical budo. / (The martial arts and ways of Japan, v. 2) /
1. Soldiers—Japan. / 2. Combat / 3. Arms and armor, Japanese / I. Title /
U43.J3D69 / 355.1'33 / 73–6613 / ISBN 978-0-8348-0234-6

CONTENTS

ACKNOWLEDGMENTS

So many people have made significant contributions to this series that to list all their names would be an impossible task. However, I wish to offer my sincere gratitude to all the headmasters and other members of the classical ryu that are either described or otherwise mentioned herein. Especially helpful to me have been Kaminoda Tsunemori, Kasegai Takashi, Otake Risuke, Otsubo Shigeo, Shiokawa Terunari, Terauchi Kenzo, Watatani Kiyoshi, translation consultants Kudo Ichiro and Takeda Hideo, and Kobayashi Ichiro and his photographic staff. I am also indebted to Dr. Benjamin A. Fusaro and Dr. John B. Hanson-Lowe for the many helpful suggestions they have made during the preparation of this manuscript.

CLASSICAL BUDO

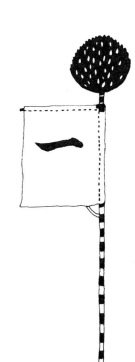

CHAPTER ONE

THE HISTORICAL SETTING

The iron hand crushed
the tyrant's head,
and became a tyrant
in his stead.

Western people are genuinely surprised to find the Japanese martial disciplines characterized as an "art" in the sense of being collectively one of the "formless expressions" of the Japanese soul, that is, expressions of the "inner man." This aspect of the martial disciplines is not readily discernible to one unfamiliar with Japanese culture, unless he is content to see these disciplines merely as clever acts that comprise an "art" of a purely physical nature. An even greater surprise awaits the Westerner when he learns of the "artless art," which far transcends mere physical skill and which can be demonstrated by the great masters of the martial disciplines.

What connection, if any, is there between the martial disciplines and the Japanese aesthetic principles of *sabi* (rusticity) and *wabi* (simplicity), in combination with pragmatic directness and the peculiar psychical quality of *kan* (intuition), that would qualify the martial disciplines to be regarded at least as "handmaids of art," if not as Japanese art forms in themselves? This important question is as yet unanswered, and a number of preconceptions and rigid beliefs about the relationship of the *bujutsu* (classical martial arts of self-protection) to the *budo* (classical martial ways of self-perfection) prevent a true understanding of these disciplines. In this book I have tried to show the classical budo in their true perspective, an approach that is empirical and conservative rather than the usual glamorized and idealistic view that originates in superficial opinions.

I have deliberately avoided giving the classical budo the popular journalistic treatment too often accorded them. I have also been careful to avoid creating the kind of shapeless mixture of fact and opinion that can so easily dominate what should be a technical discussion. I have endeavored to place the classical budo before the reader in their pure form, the existence of which is barely suspected in the Western world. The reader may then more easily see the classical disciplines in the light of their intrinsic spirit and purpose—as trials of intelligence and moral courage, and as distinctly different from the later-developed, quasi-martial, sport-oriented modern budo, such as kendo, judo, karate-do, and aiki-do. These latter forms will be treated in another volume.

The classical martial disciplines can best be understood when viewed as an integral part of the general flow of Japanese history. And so far as the classical budo are concerned, we must turn to the history of Japan prior to the Meiji Restoration of 1868 to uncover their full significance.

Man has yet to prove that he is naturally endowed with enough flexibility of mind to permit him to eliminate completely prejudices against and distrust of his fellow man. He has not yet reduced his emphasis on the improvement of the first of his primitive technologies —the making of weapons and combative systems used for the destruction of his own kind—a fact that continues to urge him to dress his political and industrial institutions in a martial manner.

Whether we believe that war is beneficial to society or that it may cause society to disintegrate, war continues to make history. It continues to be the arbiter when all else fails. Man today, as in the past, finds it necessary to label his wars, on the basis of expedient morality, as either "just" or "unjust." Both these words, however, defy attempts at universal definitions. Most decisions to wage war are based on might, not right, and rarely is war a moral issue, though rationalization seeks to make it so. For the reckless man, the horrors of war are its fascination, while for the careful man wars are counsels of despair. But we must agree with the Marquis of Montrose that "there have been wars waged to uphold decency just as there have been intervals of peace which placed comfort and profit above honour and righteous-

Samurai arming

ness." Nor is Quincy Wright amiss in his observation that though evidence of war exists in all ages, "no golden age of peace existed at any stage of human history nor did any general iron age of war." It appears, in view of the historical perspective, that there will always be men of war and men of peace, but that few are wholly of one type or the other.

The harsh realities of war always create a psychological backlash in men wearied of fighting, who then seek to promote the peaceful attributes of man through spiritual enlightenment. Japan is no exception. War weariness was the underlying reason for the creation of the classical budo, or martial ways, as distinct from their antecedents the classical bujutsu, or martial arts.

Japan as a nation was created by the interplay of a variety of complex processes in which the martial prowess of the *bushi,* the classical professional warriors, played a major role. The time from the eighth century A.D. until the end of the sixteenth century was characterized by almost constant domestic wars, which provided the bushi with opportunities to bring the bujutsu to the height of technical excellence. It was during these centuries that the bushi founded martial traditions, *ryu,* for the purpose of formalizing and perpetuating practical systems of combat.

With the founding in 1603 of the Tokugawa military government, or *bakufu,* by Tokugawa Ieyasu, warring ceased to be a dominant feature of Japanese life. The Edo period (1603–1868), in which the Tokugawa bakufu functioned, was an age favored by peace and letters. The mechanisms of Tokugawa rule cannot be adequately described briefly, but their significance in relation to the creation of the classical budo can be summarized.

Tokugawa family crest

The Tokugawa were the successors of various families who supported the military form of government called bakufu, which was originated by Minamoto Yoritomo in the late twelfth century. Tokugawa rule was virtually a dictatorship and purely aristocratic in nature. It has been described as a government that found refuge in the memory of past grandeur and one that hardened the crust of tradition and exclusiveness, while at the same time it was powerless to prevent the social and intellectual ferment that inevitably occurred when the latent energies of the people were freed by the relative peace and stability of the period. Framed within the complex structure of this government were the means that enabled the Tokugawa to retain their rule until

1868, as well as the weaknesses that helped lead to their eventual downfall.

Ieyasu and his two immediate successors as shogun spread a network of tyranny over the Japanese nation. The subtlety of their machinations shows a masterly ingenuity that is also manifest in their elaborate scheme for maintaining the ascendancy of the Tokugawa family for fourteen generations. The Tokugawa were able for a time to yoke the entire population of Japan to the immobile pillar of contentment with the status quo, soothing angered feelings and lightening depressed spirits through constant appeals to the strongest of Japanese racial traits, love for the worship of the past. The Tokugawa bakufu created the façade of a stable society in which were generated worlds within worlds, each with its separate orbit and ideas, as well as its own distinct cultural expression. The bakufu politically disarmed all potential opposition to its policies by operating as a dictatorship, and thereby cut off all internal threats of challenge to its right to rule. It both excluded Japan from the outside world and separated people within its society into rigid social classes. The Japanese people thus temporarily lost the ideal of national unity.

Training with mock spears

Its relationship with the imperial throne reveals the façade behind which the bakufu concealed its claim to the right to rule. The emperor reigned but, long devoid of all political authority, could not rule. The military guard provided by the bakufu at the Kyoto palace to protect the imperial house was, in fact, a police unit detailed to keep watch on the activities of the court aristocracy. By keeping directly under its thumb an imperial prince who had been formally invited to Edo to act as head of a temple in Ueno, the bakufu held an important noble virtual hostage.

Always, however, the bakufu showed outward respect to the throne by unceasing if meaningless ministrations. It flattered the imperial love of tradition in the unprecedented custom of the shogun's paying personal homage to the sovereign. Such homage was publicly displayed in magnificent pageants designed to remind all of the glory of Japan's martial history and of the lethal potential of the martial power of the Tokugawa bakufu—the former obvious, the latter implied. The bakufu humored the court nobles, or *kuge,* but kept them asleep in the chrysalis of tradition; it encouraged them to create and assume high-sounding but politically meaningless titles. Through the expedient of timely financial aid, the bakufu prevented the nobles from having to face the harsh realities of a decaying society. In summary, the bakufu's policy toward the imperial throne and the court was: flatter them, finance them, tire them not.

Tokugawa efforts to implement a form of government whose martial arm was wholly defensive led to the fostering of a martial spirit that was both morally hollow and technically unsound. This spirit finally destroyed the society that it was originally intended to serve. The bakufu discouraged martial imagination and inventiveness and in the long run proved hostile to the development and maintenance of martial skill. It also created a society of privileged, idle armed men who were restless in unproductive service.

The warrior class was divided into cleverly conceived groups and brought under control through the establishment of hundreds of feudal demesnes called *han*. These were so situated that martial alliances among those warriors most likely to prove hostile to the bakufu were impossible. The bakufu positioned its most trusted bushi and their domains between those of the warriors it distrusted most, making of the former buffers against subversion. The daimyo, the grandees who ruled the han and who mustered bushi in support of their domains, were required by the bakufu to go to Edo periodically to sit in attendance on the shogun. This practice, *sankin kotai*, obligated each daimyo to leave his home province every other year and to invest vast sums of money for the privilege of living in Edo in an extravagant style. The families of the daimyo were required to reside permanently in Edo, virtual hostages of the bakufu. Thus the daimyo were continually draining their feudatory incomes and spending the greater portion of their lives making journeys to and from their home provinces. This was a policy well calculated by the bakufu to give no opportunity to the powerful daimyo to be hostile to Tokugawa rule in more than thought.

Jealousy and rivalry among daimyo competing for Tokugawa favor was encouraged by the bakufu, which pretended to extend equal opportunity to all. From the seeds of distrust among daimyo grew a constant state of espionage and counterespionage within the domains of all daimyo. Because of its strategy of dissipating the strength of the daimyo, the bakufu was led to expect and accept occasional brawls between the men of rival daimyo. Classical bushi were outnumbered by masses of conscript soldiers taken from lower social ranks; these soldiers relied

Staff training with mask

upon firearms. Hand-to-hand combat, which had been based on high moral and technically excellent principles—a quick wrist, a keen eye, and moral courage—in the days when all Japan was a martial camp, was now for the most part relegated to the shadowy realm of history and tradition.

Tokugawa rule was patriarchal and sometimes benevolent toward its privileged warrior class; but it was also despotic. Daimyo who might chance a revolt against the bakufu would soon find to their chagrin just how impotent they really were in martial matters. Punished for their crimes against the feudal state by having their territories cut down, transferred, or confiscated, thwarted daimyo formulated policies of espionage and intrigue among themselves that infected the whole bushi complex with a consuming suspicion of itself. Rival daimyo factions were involved in a continuous series of undercover struggles for power. A daimyo's sphere of influence depended on a delicate balance of power not infrequently determined by an insidious unscrupulousness.

Tokugawa bushi, generally referred to as samurai, were required to serve under the shogun or with the various daimyo in the provinces. Some of these bushi stemmed from the highest-ranking classical warrior families, or *buke*, but others rose from lower social strata through cunning or circumstance. But all bushi now expected to attain and maintain their privileged social position by birthright rather than by long service in combat, which had been the criterion of the classical bushi of earlier periods. With no war to be fought, this expectation became custom, and because of it the martial quality of the Tokugawa bushi deteriorated.

The bakufu required the bushi to submit their unruly spirits to a quasi-martial routine tinctured with a modicum of academic learning. The scope of the bujutsu was reduced from what had been customary prior to Tokugawa rule; some Tokugawa shogun even ordered martial training to cease altogether. In place of the bujutsu the bushi were expected to take part in tea ceremony, dancing, singing, acting, the composition of poetry, and various other nonmartial activities. A Confucian-oriented education was ordered for the bushi in the belief that its ethical basis would diminish martial ardor and encourage the worship of tradition for its own sake. Obligations came to outweigh rights, and the Tokugawa bushi found themselves in an ethical straitjacket, bound by convention.

Tea-ceremony whisk

The only bushi who escaped this straitjacket were those known as *ronin:* bushi who owed loyalty to no superior. Through extinction of a daimyo domain, release from professional obligations, or personal choice, a bushi might become a ronin. Though he retained all the rights and privileges of the ordinary bushi who was attached to some organ within the bakufu, he also exercised the right to express his private opinions to a degree unknown among his orthodox counterparts.

Bakufu policy toward its warriors can be summarized thus: glorify them, divert their martial energies, keep them financially obligated. This policy made the bushi warriors in only a nominal sense.

Among the commoners, strangely enough, the bakufu found good allies against ambitious daimyo. Consequently, the bakufu granted commoners many privileges hitherto unknown. They were allowed virtual self-government in certain well-defined spheres in which industry, agriculture, and commerce flourished—but not without Tokugawa exploitation of the revenues derived therefrom. Severe taxation of the incomes that the commoners derived from their enterprises provided the means whereby the bakufu supported its feudal governmental structure. Moreover, in spite of some concessions to commoners, the bakufu pursued a policy of requiring them to live in a closed social compartment. They were welcome to their own special vocations and amusements but forbidden to trespass on what the bakufu regarded as the realm of those socially superior to commoners, the nobles and the warriors. On public signboards the commoners found such succinct advice as the following: "Each person must devote himself to his own business, without negligence, and in all respects keep within the limits proper to his social position."

A commoner was strictly forbidden to wear the *daisho* (two swords, one long and one short) of the bushi, though certain commoner officials might wear a single medium-length sword. Citizens in general were unarmed. No commoner was permitted to display a family crest on his clothing or property; in fact, he was not even allowed to bear a surname. Commoners could have their Kabuki theater but might not indulge in watching the Gagaku court dances or the Noh drama that were so popular with the nobles and bushi. All literary and art forms were permitted to commoners, so long as they were not subversive in the opinion of the bakufu. An immense body of police spies maintained constant surveillance, alert to any violation of bakufu regulations in

Young stalwart with two swords

either spirit or deed. Those suspected of violating these regulations were quickly rounded up and subjected to interrogation.

Under Tokugawa criminal law the only valid proof of guilt was the accused's own confession in writing, formally sealed by him. Not until this was obtained could he be sentenced. When the ordinary methods of browbeating and intimidation failed to obtain a confession, torture was the legal recourse, a practice that became increasingly common in the later years of the Tokugawa regime. A suspect might be subjected to four degrees of torture in order to make him confess guilt. The usual methods, in order of increasing severity, were the following: 1) Scourging, which consisted of binding the suspect and beating him with split-bamboo rods (*madake*). 2) "Hugging the stone," whereby the suspect was bound and made to sit in a formal kneeling posture (*seiza*) on a platform of three-cornered hardwood planks positioned with sharp edges uppermost; the suspect was securely fastened to this platform while heavy stone slabs were piled on his thighs. 3) "The lobster," which consisted of twisting the suspect's arms in a painful manner and tying them so that they were behind the back and pulled up to the shoulders; then the legs were tied together in front of the body and pulled up to the chin, at which moment the front and back of the body were pulled tightly together and bound with a rope of hard twisted hemp. 4) Suspension, in which the suspect had his arms pinned to his sides, hands tied behind his back, and was hoisted by means of a rope fastened around his wrists to a beam overhead; the suspect's toes dangled only inches from the ground. If convicted of a crime, the commoner might face punishments that ranged from simple humiliation by tattooing, to exile, to such grim horrors as decapitation, crucifixion, or burning at the stake.

The bakufu policy toward its common people may be summarized as follows: amuse them, abuse them, don't tell them anything.

Below the rank of commoner were those called *hinin,* "nonhumans," who were regarded as subhuman. They were completely ostracized from Tokugawa society. Their menial functions included acting as jailers, executioners, torturers, and corpse handlers for the bakufu. Others were recruited as *ninja,* supersleuth espionage agents.

The form of government adopted by the first Tokugawa shogun, Ieyasu, was relatively loose-knit, and its functions were carried out by men who made cautious decisions. It remained for Ieyasu's two imme-

Ninja *climbing a rope*

diate successors to bring close organization to the bakufu. But considering the policies of these three Tokugawa martial men, it is evident that all three were determined to maintain the peace by means of an absolute state governed in perpetuity by the Tokugawa family. In their capable hands the bakufu served as the mechanism by which the country made the difficult transition from an age of war to an age of peace.

One of the most important problems facing the bakufu was control of the professional warrior class of bushi. The *Buke Sho-Hatto*, "Rules for Martial Families," a document whose thirteen clauses set out rules of conduct for martial families, was drawn up in 1615 on Ieyasu's order by the Zen priest Suden in collaboration with other scholars. The document opened with this first, all-important injunction: "Literary arts [*bun*], weapons [*buki*], *kyujutsu* [archery], and *bajutsu* [horsemanship] are to be the regular and favorite pursuits.

"Putting literary arts first and martial arts [*bu*] next was the custom of our ancestors. These subjects must be cultivated concurrently. Kyujutsu and bajutsu are the most essential for the buke. Weapons of war are ill-omened words to utter; the use of them, however, is an unavoidable necessity. In times of peace and good order we must not forget that disturbances may arise. Dare we omit the practice of our martial arts?"

Ieyasu's *Buke Sho-Hatto* clearly gives priority to martial studies, and for that reason, through the term of office of the third shogun, Iemitsu (ruled 1623–51), the bakufu remained essentially a martial government. Iemitsu himself was an expert swordsman and was thoroughly devoted to the classical warrior's way of life. He made his position known in uncompromising terms upon his succession to the office of shogun: "My ancestor [Ieyasu] and his son [Hidetada] regarded you as equals, and you have had special privileges. But now I am shogun by right of succession, and you will henceforth be treated as ordinary hereditary subjects. If you do not like this, go back to your domains and think carefully about what I have said. Then, as tradition dictates, the clash of arms shall decide who is to be supreme in this country." The warrior class did nothing to evoke Iemitsu's wrath.

Iemitsu's revision of the first article of Ieyasu's *Buke Sho-Hatto* in 1635 was also bold, but more succinct: "The taste for the Way of literature, weapons, kyujutsu, and bajutsu is to be the chief object of cultivation."

After Iemitsu's death in 1651, nonmartial trends in policy and personal weaknesses in the shogun made the bakufu a martial government

"Hugging the stone"

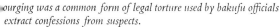

...ourging was a common form of legal torture used by bakufu officials ...extract confessions from suspects.

A more painful form of torture was the method of binding called "the lobster."

in name only. Henceforth, on the occasion of a succession to the office of shogun, considerable changes and amendments were written into the *Buke Sho-Hatto*. By the time of Tsunayoshi, the fifth shogun (ruled 1680–1709), the balance between the martial and academic aspects of the original first clause had been upset. It now read (1683): "Literature and weapons, loyalty and filial piety should be earnestly cultivated, and ceremonial decorum and rectitude be correctly observed."

Tsunayoshi's successor, Ienobu (ruled 1709–13), in his 1710 revision of the *Buke Sho-Hatto*, further reduced the martial impact of the first clause: "The Way of literature and weapons must be constantly pursued; but [more important], social strata must be clearly distinguished and manners [appropriate to each] must be correctly followed [by all persons]."

These changes reflect the influence of the Neo-Confucian doctrine that provided the Tokugawa bakufu with an ethical sanction for its policies. By the promulgation of selected principles of orthodox Chu Hsi Neo-Confucianism, with its emphasis on filial piety and social decorum, the bakufu hoped to stabilize the social order. But antagonism to the bakufu's brand of Confucianism arose in several quarters, and social and economic disturbances also threatened that hope for stability. From the clash of opinions that followed there evolved an intellectual ferment that greatly influenced the course of Japanese history. It was against this background that the classical budo developed.

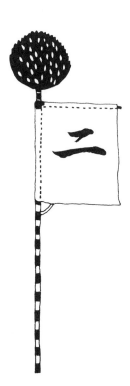

CHAPTER TWO

THE CONCEPT

That way over the mountain,
which who stands upon,
Is apt to doubt if it be
indeed a road.
               Robert Browning

The classical budo is one of the products of the intellectual ferment that eventually broke down the narrow limits within which the Confucian-oriented bakufu officials sought to confine the thinking of the Japanese people. Ironically, it was the very Confucianism which the bakufu hoped would provide social strictures for its citizens that stimulated them to tug at the handles of the locked doors holding their minds captive. A trend toward greater independence in thought grew increasingly marked throughout the eighteenth century, the inevitable result of the craving of the majority of Edo-period citizens for new outlets for their energies and talents in a time of peace.

Bakufu officials used their scholarship to draw up a list of orthodox concepts that were later given the sanction of the government. It was the Neo-Confucianism of the eminent Sung-dynasty philosopher Chu Hsi (1130–1200) that was chosen to serve as the basis of bakufu Confucianism. Chu Hsi's socially oriented philosophy, called Tei-shu or Shu-shi in Japanese, was well suited to the purposes of the bakufu. It was concerned with humanism, in the sense that it focused directly on man and his closest human relationships rather than upon spiritual or divine law. This philosophy stressed man's obligation to fulfill the loyalties demanded by filial piety, social relationships, and his duty as a subject to his ruler.

But the dominance of the Chu Hsi system in Japan was far from complete. Rivaling the bakufu orthodoxy was the Wang Yang-ming (1472–1529) system of Confucianism, called Oyomei in Japanese. Its teachings were completely personal and stressed reliance upon intuition and moral sense rather than upon the intellect as in Chu Hsi's doctrine. It is dedication to systematic physical endeavor, Wang Yang-ming Confucianism maintains, that teaches man to control his mind, and that is the only "true learning." Through such a learning process man aims at "exemplifying illustrious virtue." In the unity of knowledge and action imposed by self-discipline, man can arrive at a level of self-understanding unattainable by any other means. The Wang Yang-ming system can be seen to be similar to Zen philosophy in a number of respects. Like Zen, both the system and its methods of spiritual cultivation are simple and direct, qualities that gave it a powerful appeal to warriors.

In its insistence on action rather than words, Wang Yang-ming Confucianism urged man to assert himself and to improve his life. This position, which favored individual merit over hereditary privilege, naturally alarmed the bakufu, which was based so firmly on hereditary position. Both the Wang Yang-ming system and its many advocates were severely criticized by the bakufu, and in some instances its exponents were exiled in an attempt to silence their dangerous thoughts. The bakufu maintained that the developer of this "misguided part of philosophy," Wang Yang-ming, had one serious defect as a scholar: his passionate love for the study of martial tactics and strategy. Hayashi Razan (1583–1657), Confucian tutor to the shogun, wrote: "True gentleman do not devote themselves to this kind of study."

According to Chinese philosophy, increasing knowledge—information about matters of fact—is not the highest goal of human endeavor. Rather, it is the elevation of the mind, a reaching out for what lies beyond the "present self," that is to be sought. In this formal and idealistic sense the individual reveres values that are higher than merely moral ones, values that are "supramoral." In the *Lao-tzu* (a work thought to contain the precepts of the ancient philosopher Lao Tzu, and later called the *Tao Te Ching*), one of the great classics of Chinese literature, is the statement: "To work on learning is to increase day by day; to work on Tao is to decrease day by day."

The former kind of work is a conceptual endeavor that concerns the increase of positive knowledge through reason or principle (*li*); the latter emphasizes the elevation of the mind (*hsin*) through participation in physical endeavor. The apparent paradox between what the Chinese

Kamae *with sword*

regard as the "highest goal" of human endeavor and the manner of attaining it, prescribed in the passage quoted above from the *Lao-tzu,* is resolved when one realizes that the *Lao-tzu* also states: "Diminish a thing and it will increase; increase a thing and it will dimish."

The *Chuang-tzu,* another Chinese classic (traditionally attributed to Chuang Tzu, 369?–286? B.C.) available to Japanese scholars, makes a strong plea for the spiritual freedom of the individual. The *Chuang-tzu,* though less concerned with establishing the Tao as a guide for human life, nevertheless dwells on the mystical process by which man can rise above mundane affairs.

Tao, according to both the *Lao-tzu* and the *Chuang-tzu,* is nameless and unnameable, a unitary "that" from which all else springs. Such is the orthodox Taoist view. The Japanese, however, less inclined than the Chinese to abstract speculations about an "otherwordly" life, and favoring a pragmatic outlook, took the Tao—*Dō* in Japanese—to be a more realistic concept, one that was applicable to man in his social relationships. They preferred the Confucian interpretation of the Tao as a nameable, named, and multiple concept that nevertheless transcends both nature and man.

Tao (dō, michi)

The basis for what the Japanese call *dō* or *michi,* "way," lies in these ancient concepts of the Tao carried to Japan from China. Whatever the original meanings for the Chinese, they were modified both by native Japanese beliefs like Shinto and by the social and political requirements of the ruling elite, who synthesized from these Chinese elements a pattern of thought compatible with Japanese feudal society.

Behind the philosophical and ethical essence of the dō are found religious undertones, but the dō is not a religion in itself. A spirit of religiousness exists in the dō only in the sense that the concept stems from a superstructure of Chinese classical studies based on superstitions, rituals, and institutions. The essentially nonreligious outlook of the Japanese people did not add to the dō in this sphere; their high degree of absorption in human relationships prevented this.

The Tao as dō was therefore understood by the Japanese to be a "way" or "road" to follow in life. That way is endless and profound. It is long, steep, and filled with numerous technical difficulties. It is to be traveled as a means of self-cultivation, and it leads ultimately to self-perfection.

The concept of the dō is protean. It embraces a variety of practical, activistic disciplines, or dō forms, closely associated with Japanese secular life. All these disciplines are complicated, intricate challenges in the pursuit of a better way of life, and are based on the firm conviction that no man is as complete a human being as he can be after sufficient experience with the dō.

A dō form may be thought of as the product of the connection that links philosophy and its ethical applications. The implication is that the "way" rests on a spiritual foundation that is expressed and lived through training in a prescribed manner directed toward an ideal of human behavior, which, in turn, elevates the individual and thus the society in which he lives. All dō forms aim to remove traditional prejudices from human relationships. Moral character is taken to be the measure of a man, for if character cannot be depended upon, it is believed, no man-made system can be valid. Because the dō forms train man to be "more human," they are also considered to be the "true path of humanity," an application of living knowledge that is manifested in acts of assistance to other human beings. The dō are, therefore, the exemplification of man's faith in cultural humanism.

The cultural objective of the dō forms is to enable a man to be simply and naturally a man, without ostentation, affectation, or self-consciousness, and thus lead him to engage in wholesome relationships with others. Metaphysically speaking, the dō forms urge their advocates to seek an understanding of the whole of life through a segment of it, a sphere of personal activity in which the cadence of nature can be sensed and experienced. The dō forms thus involve transferring an attitude toward life from the particular to the universal and absolute.

The dō forms are indissolubly tied to Zen. They are, in fact, plastic Zen. They are the means by which Zen is kept in touch with everyday life. At the same time, they act only as the vehicles by which the individual can reach his goal, only "helps" toward that last decisive "leap to enlightenment" that culminates in self-perfection. According to Zen concepts, the worst obstacle to self-perfection is self-deception. The dō prevent self-deception. The achievement of self-perfection, the "enlightened" state, in a dō form can be judged only by masters of the dō. It is impossible to simulate this state of being.

Enlightenment, *satori,* is a state of being in which self-perfection is more important to the person who possesses it than are his motor skills. What is accomplished in the execution of a physical technique presup-

Satori

poses more than simply perfected physical skill. Any action well performed as physical technique alone fails to be mastery if the performer's state of mind is tense and he exhibits consciousness of his actions. He is a technician, perhaps a master of technique, but not a master of himself. He controls physical skill admirably but does not fully control himself. Compared to the master, his actions are spasmodic; those of the master are "unintentional," taking place as naturally as ripened fruit drops from the tree. The master's movements always appear to be "effortless effort" or "artless art." All techniques, a great river flowing incessantly, have been learned by the master through painstaking experience. The technician's skill, on the other hand, is simply a river with a temporary flow after a heavy rainfall, soon exhausted. Whereas the master's actions guarantee appropriate results, those of the technician fail to do so.

Mastery of the dō is wisdom, while learning pursued only for the sake of knowledge falls short of wisdom. The bujutsu depend largely on technical knowledge but express contempt for the conceptual method of arriving at such knowledge—achieving an understanding of a subject primarily through dependence upon words—in the maxim: "To know and to act are one and the same." It is practice, not theory, that is to be sought. Learning is accomplished by doing a thing and living it out, making it part of one's daily life. Further, the doing must be accomplished through the use of the processes of mind (*shin*), which, when integrated, activate the "inner light," or intuition (*kan*).

Fudoshin

The activistic spirit of the bujutsu is evident in this process of learning through actions, not words. This is a psychological kind of learning. For the bujutsu, logical learning (dependence upon words) is a rapid, short-term process that produces shallow knowledge (no understanding of the self, and not always practical), whereas psychological learning is of a slow, long-term nature and produces the deep knowledge (understanding of the self, and always practical) that leads to true wisdom.

The concept of the dō, as attached to the classical martial disciplines in the sixteenth century, placed full reliance upon the psychological method of learning but amplified its principle. Famed *kenshi* (expert swordsmen), such as Tsukahara Bokuden (1490–1571), placed emphasis on matters other than those concerned with expertise in physical technique. Bokuden wrote of a "growing from within," suggesting the necessity of developing in warriors a spiritual power that he designated "the core of mastery." He noted that such mastery appears to yield like a "curtain surrendering to the force of a stone striking it" only to resist, finally, then "contain its enemy and defeat it."

The concept of dō implies harmony. Though spiritual power is operative in all people, it is brought to its maximum by those who are in harmony with nature. One way a person may harmonize himself with nature is through his dedication to a dō form. Such dedication means beginning with a high degree of physical activity, for no understanding of the dō, let alone mastery, is possible by any other means. Inactivity is to be exchanged for relentless participation in prescribed disciplines in order to obtain firsthand experience by doing. The dō forms thus came to be thought of as "understanding," or "understanding what, whom, self." The great swordsman Yagyu Tajima no Kami (1527–1606) expresses this best:

"Learning and knowledge are meant to be 'forgotten,' and it is only when this is realized that you feel perfectly comfortable. . . . However well a man may be trained in the art [*kenjutsu*], the swordsman can never be the master of his technical knowledge unless all his psychical hindrances are removed and he can keep the mind in the state of emptiness [*mu*], purged even of whatever technique he has obtained. The entire body together with the four limbs will then be capable of displaying for the first time and to its full extent all the art acquired by the training of several years. The body will move as if automatically, with no conscious effort on the part of the swordsman himself. . . . All the training is there, but the mind [shin] is utterly unconscious of it. The mind does not know where it is. When this is realized, with all the training thrown to the winds, with a mind perfectly unaware of its own workings, with the self vanished nowhere anybody knows, the art of swordsmanship attains its perfection and one who has it is called a *meijin*."

Kenshi

The master of the dō form, the meijin, is a technician whose ability goes far beyond that of simple physical expertise. His essence is a spiritual one. Self-perfection is his salient characteristic; he has gone beyond the "doing and seeking" levels of training. But the meijin is a living example of an ordered, disciplined life. He continues to make great demands on himself and never omits daily training.

The meijin is recognized through the atmosphere of tranquillity that surrounds him. He possesses *fudoshin,* or "immovable mind," a mental state that enables him to meet any situation with composure. Circum-

Kenjutsu

stances that produce varying degrees of shock in ordinary men—such as a loud and unexpected noise—fail to register on the master's prevailing outward calm and attest to the depth of his ease of mind. Any action of the meijin reflects the dominance of his mind over his body in the controlled efficiency of his movements. He has an agile body that moves in a characteristically light and accurate fashion when training, and his movements bear the quality of "accident": he does things in such a way that it is as though they happen accidentally. This quality cannot be gained through analysis, masterful mimicry, or an assumed attitude of expediency; it is entirely due to the spontaneous functioning of the self. The high state of mastery over technique and self tunes the meijin's mind to such a degree of sensitivity that his body is responsive to the slightest need for action in order to avoid danger. It is also this state of mind that allows the meijin to rise above the petty self to a state of selflessness, or "no-self" (selfishness removed). Therefore the meijin is always a humble man whose fine manners and courtesy give him great dignity. He stands as proof of the value of wholesome human endeavor gained through experience in facing the rigors of self-imposed discipline.

Muga-mushin,
"no-self"

For the meijin, the protracted discipline of a classical dō culminates in a special kind of spiritual strength unattainable by those who do not engage in such disciplines. The performance of the meijin can be likened to the fragrance of a flower; it can only suggest, never be, the flower itself, which is its source. An ordinary exponent of dō disciplines does not know any more than he has learned or can express in action; but as he acquires mastery, first of technique, then of himself, his insight quickens and deepens, and there are qualities that he unconsciously suggests rather than consciously exhibits.

One of these qualities is summed up in the expression *kan-ken futatsu no koto*. Originally, as used by warriors in connection with the bujutsu, it signified a desirable attribute in the warrior's makeup, a subliminal sense in which both (futatsu no koto) the eyes and the mind (kan-ken) served as mechanisms of "sight" in times of danger. *Ken wa me de miru*—ordinary sight (ken) relies on and is only as good as the eyes (me)—but *kan wa kokoro*, the intuitive mind (kan) is the heart (kokoro) of seeing. For the warrior, *ken no me wa yowaku*, sight by means of the eyes was weak and unreliable; but *kan no me wa tsuyoi*, seeing into the heart by means of intuition was strong and reliable. The former is physical sight, limited to perceiving movement or performance; the latter is psychical sight, which penetrates to the essence.

The warrior, in his application of bujutsu, used the expression "kan-ken futatsu no koto" to denote a kind of awareness that gave him the ability to adapt himself expertly and unconsciously to dangerous situations. For example, this ability might be evident in his manner of effectively and simultaneously dealing with two foes, one of whom menaced him from the front, the other from the rear. The combatant saw the former through his physical eyes, the latter through his mental "eyes." The same expression might be used to describe the uncanny ability of the warrior to utilize small things to his advantage, such as gaining a toehold in a small depression in the ground behind him, which he could not see, so as to move more quickly and powerfully against a foe. The same ability to use his mental "eyes" enabled the warrior to step instantly over a log, body, or rock lying out of sight behind him in the path of his backward movement.

Used in connection with the classical budo forms, however, the expression kan-ken futatsu no koto has instead a spiritual meaning, that of seeing (ken) and understanding (kan) the inner self.

The absence of kan-ken futastu no koto in trainees is irrefutable evidence of their lack of experience and, consequently, of the fact that they have not yet attained meijin status. The novice, for example, is completely inexperienced, therefore he sees only with his eyes. He copies his master's performance and imitates it without knowing the principles behind it. The master regards the novice as being without either height or depth of maturity, in a technical sense. A trainee who is more skilled, however, has ability in a number of individual techniques that he can perform without watching his master. Yet, though the master concedes that this trainee has some height (number of techniques), which is visible, it is evident to the master that depth (maturation), which is invisible, is lacking. As long as the trainee must depend for success on imitating his master, he is without mastery even if his mimicry is perfect. Not until the trainee makes his performance his own can he properly be recognized as a meijin. To imitate is but performance; to have achieved true resemblance is essence.

Because the meijin possesses a high level of skill and represents a person who has achieved something that is supernormal—self-perfection—he is sometimes also referred to as a *kami*. "Kami" is a word that

Kami

etymologically evokes a number of meanings, among which are "deity," "god," "legendary hero," and "something or someone possessing strange or extraordinary powers." But there is more than this to the meaning of kami. The *ka* sound implies hidden, mystical, invisible, and intangible properties, while the *mi* sound implies fullness or maturity. The meijin, or kami, is believed to be a divinely inspired person, one who has direct contact with things "otherworldly," as evidenced, to give only one example, in his ability to guarantee the perfect result during the performance of a technique.

But the meijin is not infallible. He can and does make mistakes. The Japanese have a saying illustrating this: *Ki kara saru mo ochiru,* "Even monkeys fall out of trees." There is thus a permitted, even expected, degree of lack of mastery in the master, as shown in those rare instances when he actually commits some technical error in the performance of a technique. But the master actually makes merits even of such errors. By a curious mixture of nonerror and error the master demonstrates his virtuosity. A less skilled exponent, on committing an error, will terminate his performance at that point because the threads of movement and spirit in the performance have been severed; he is unable to join them together. The master, however, immediately after making an error, without hesitation continues his original course of action and follows it to its intended conclusion; he is able to pick up and instantly weave together the severed threads. So subtle is the break in rhythm caused by the error that usually only another master can recognize the fact that there has been an error at all. In this way, although accidentally having made a mistake, the master (kami) confirms the fact that he is not devoid of human qualities.

Kan-ken

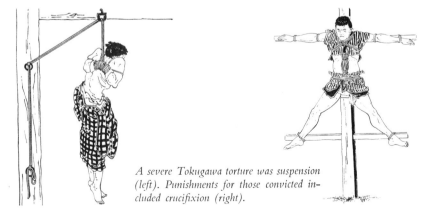

A severe Tokugawa torture was suspension (left). Punishments for those convicted included crucifixion (right).

ALE

e known to the Japa-
hinese meant a vari-
he administration of
ts; they further sug-
academic and mar-

Originally the Japanese seem to have accepted the Chinese meaning, but after the Kamakura period (1185–1336) the meaning of budo in Japan narrowed, coming to indicate the process of ruling the nation through martial power. During the violence that characterized the period extending from the mid-fourteenth century to the end of the sixteenth century, the meaning of the term "budo" included cultivation of the virtues of the classical warrior and of certain ethical values of the then-inchoate *bushido,* the warrior code. The virtues of loyalty and courage, which were sometimes displayed on the field of combat, were idealized. These virtues and others were made the basis of the indomitable spirit of the classical warrior, whose primary concern was to achieve the state of *seishi o choetsu*—"transcending life and death"— that is, a frame of mind in which one is able to transcend thoughts of life and death. It was the classical warrior's mental preparation, his breaking through the spiritual border between life and death, that gave rise to a spiritual awakening in him. Edo-period warrior-intellectuals, such as Daidoji Yuzan, who wrote *Budo Shoshin-shu* (Martial Ways Primer) in 1686, confirmed that the essence of budo was synonymous with the ethical code of the classical warriors. Thus the spiritual and ethical concepts of the classical warrior became an intrinsic part of classical budo.

The bushi, troubled with eternal restlessness, sought constantly for spiritual renewal and a balm beyond the human realm for spiritual fatigue. The commoner, too, oppressed by the social tyranny of the Tokugawa bakufu, searched for ways out of his straitjacket. Both bushi and commoner, though socially segregated, at this time became acutely aware of their existence as individuals and of the limitations of their respective spheres, and began to question the significance of their innermost feelings.

Greater self-abnegation and identification with nature were demanded of the bushi than were necessary for men who did not follow the profession of arms. A man who is unable to cultivate or has not cultivated this harmony with nature is easily brutalized and coarsened. In the end, it is the extent to which he is able to harmonize his essence with nature that determines whether or not he will be capable of humane acts or will remain forever vulnerable to the human tendency to behave barbarously. The commoner, for his part, sought self-respect through competence in doing something creative that would give him a sense of worthwhile accomplishment.

Bushido

Bushi and commoner alike sought the frivolities of life, the loneliness of religion, or such solace as could be found in the pursuit of the mysterious and unknown, in their attempts to forget their essential boredom with life. But their entertainments afforded them little more than temporary relief, and religion, while it might soothe men's minds, could not cure the spiritual malaise. The lives of Edo-period men lacked an area of true spirituality, leaving them bereft of something wholly spiritual in which to put their faith. In this spiritual vacuum, expressions of spiritual freedom evinced through faith in the unknown brought to many of these barren lives that which they sought most— some moisture to the aridity of life, a psychological thirst-quencher. One expression of spiritual freedom was the creation of the budo, the martial ways.

The creation of the classical budo was indicated by the nominal change of the ideogram for *jutsu,* "art," in the word "bujutsu" to *dō,* "way." This change heralded men's desire to cultivate an awareness of their spiritual nature through the exercise of disciplines that would bring them to a state of self-realization. It is this goal that underlies the major difference between a classical martial discipline labeled "jutsu" and one termed "dō."

The bujutsu, or martial arts, developed from crude beginnings concerned largely with technical achievements. But as the need and concern for combative techniques lessened in the Tokugawa period, the "art" stage of "forgetting technique" and "forgetting self" (discussed in detail in Chapter 4) emerged. This is the level of the dō. Yagyu Tajima no Kami expressed the ethic of this stage: "All weapons meant to kill are inauspicious, and must never be used except on occasions of extreme urgency. If any at all is to be used, however, let it be known that it is only for the purpose of punishing evils and not for depriving one of life. To understand this, learning is the first requisite. But mere learning will never do. It is an entrance gate through which one is to proceed to the residence proper to interview the master himself. The master is Tao, truth."

Though they stemmed from the technical basis of bujutsu, the classical budo were not designed to serve the warrior in combat. Certain, but not all, of the bujutsu were modified for budo training by recasting them in a metaphysical mold. Whereas the bujutsu emphasized form to be used for bringing about an effective combative result, the budo stressed form to be used as a means for gaining an understanding of the self, of being, and of nature, and for gaining self-perfection. Training in budo thus, it was believed, aimed at "higher values" than those of bujutsu.

Bujutsu

Because they were born in a period of peace and were not required to stand the test of combat, the majority of the developers of the budo assumed that nothing essential would be suppressed by waiving the combative ends of the bujutsu. Many bushi were repelled at the evolution of a bujutsu form to that of its budo counterpart. But the very fact that other bushi advocated this great change in purpose is significant evidence of the growing sense of awareness in the Japanese people that men ought to live in peace.

The classical budo forms were created by active people for active people, all of whom sought to relate creative activities to the ideals of the past. The classical budo, like the bujutsu, were therefore deeply rooted in the culture of feudal-age Japan. It should be understood, however, that the budo were not created as forms of social amusement or

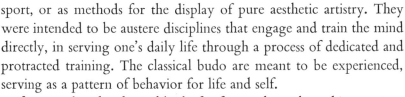

Iai-do

Seiza *posture*

sport, or as methods for the display of pure aesthetic artistry. They were intended to be austere disciplines that engage and train the mind directly, in serving one's daily life through a process of dedicated and protracted training. The classical budo are meant to be experienced, serving as a pattern of behavior for life and self.

If one studies the classical budo for fun or through a whim, no true understanding is possible. The goal of self-perfection requires time and effort, and direction is always more important than haste. The founders of the classical budo systems prescribed certain disciplines to open the mind's eye. These disciplines are akin to pure introspective mysticism; one can only enter mystic experience through direct participation. This law of participation, which all the classical disciplines obey, allows no exception. The classical budo disclose their meaning only to those who are dedicated and who exert their minds and bodies in rigorous training. To others, the "way," or dō—the "fire of truth"—is always closed. And even to those who have "entered," many years of stoic training are necessary for a true appreciation of the meaning of the classical budo.

The founders of the classical budo regarded form as an active force in man's daily life. They selected and adapted certain aspects of form developed earlier by the classical bushi for use in bujutsu. Their adaptation was not haphazard. These founders were creative geniuses. The specific actions in the techniques used in budo disciplines that they chose were those most likely to lead to intense concentration. Every movement was regarded as the natural expression of a man in action. All were delicately interconnected in such a way that should one of the major elements be removed, the resulting action would be greatly weakened as a means of gaining spiritual perfection.

The discipline of swordsmanship in *iai-do* fashion provides an easily understood example of the intense concentration demanded by budo techniques. The trainee must, in the final stage of wielding the sword, return its razor-sharp blade to the scabbard he wears at his left hip. The action used in accomplishing this brings the operator's left hand within a fraction of an inch of the keen edge, in itself an unnerving maneuver for the untrained, but one made infinitely more delicate by the fact that the action must be performed without once looking at the scabbard. This dangerous moment is made safe and successful only by applying intuitive (kan) "feel."

It is an error to consider the classical budo forms a religion. Neither

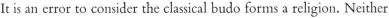

are they ceremony or ritual, that is, a specialized vehicle for the exercise of etiquette; nor do they comprise acts of cleverness and dexterity carried out for religious or ceremonial purposes. It is true that the classical budo are concerned with what amounts to a religious—that is, devoted —adherence to the mechanical aspects of form, but their greater purpose is to draw the bow, to wield the sword or other weapons, in a spiritual manner. These weapons must be used spiritually, the foremost thought being "one shot, one life." If this premise is lacking, then all action is empty of meaning.

The essence of the classical bushi's conventional rules of behavior lay in self-protection. But such etiquette was only a secondary consideration, an exercise in poise and deportment. If this is not understood, the classical bujutsu are meaningless, an empty cultivation of form. For example, when the classical warrior knelt first on his left knee in the process of adopting a sitting-kneeling (*seiza*) or crouching (*iai-goshi*) posture, a matter of form to which he never made exception, he did so in order to be able rapidly to draw his sword, which was carried or worn at his left side, should it become necessary to do so. As he sat, his beautiful posture was conditioned by the very practical fact that it permitted him to move as quickly as possible if danger threatened him. And when he rose to a standing position, his right knee would precede his left knee in a way that allowed him to draw his blade unhindered.

The founders of the classical budo systems tended to ignore the combative meanings behind the warriors' use of physical form and etiquette; while adopting the warriors' mannerisms, they made etiquette, not utility, paramount. Courtesy is as important as demeanor in the performance of classical budo techniques because it develops into the elegance of refined movement and tranquillity, and is related to the cultivation of the total man. In their insistence on correct physical form, in terms of both technique and etiquette, the exponents of the classical budo forms ensured that they would achieve self-discipline of the highest order.

Though classical budo are concerned with physical form, and exist only in theory if form is discarded, form is but the physical or visual element of budo. There is also a spiritual element that must be recognized. Form is only the materialization of the spirit, thus it is characteristic of the classical budo disciplines to look behind form for its essence. Form is the framework of that which rises from it—the activity of the

Sword-drawing

spirit; to dispense with form means that there is nothing left to serve its master, the spirit. Mastery of form is but a point, though an important one, to be sure, along the "way." In the end form is discarded and the final stage of personal development—self-perfection—is achieved.

The classical budo are evidence of the evolution of techniques based on common sense and centuries of practical combat experience to the level of peaceful "ways of life." The Confucian ethical outlook on social organization is found in the budo systems in their emphasis on the social responsibilities of man. From Taoist elements the budo emphasize what is natural and spontaneous in him. The budo thus serve as the vehicles of both moral and supramoral education. As such the budo are considered to be not instruments for killing but vehicles through which individuals can aspire to moral perfection. This emphasis on the moral sphere of human activities is an outstanding feature of the classical budo. Though the classical bujutsu and budo share a concern for morality, differences in the priority accorded moral acts distinguish them. If the classical bujutsu and budo are considered as three-dimensional forms, the following priorities hold:

> classical bujutsu: 1) combat, 2) discipline, 3) morals
> classical budo: 1) morals, 2) discipline, 3) aesthetic form

Miyabi

Social changes during the Edo period made possible the emergence of the classical budo. With these changes, what had previously served as training for battle (bujutsu) for the aristocratic few (the classical warriors) was modified so that it became suitable and available as the basis for a system of training for everyday life (budo) for common men.

During the Edo period, criteria for aesthetic principles set by new standards of taste were established. These standards, however, did not represent a sharp break with the past but were instead extensions and intensifications of older ideals. Japanese creative artists throughout the ages have used special words to indicate their canons of taste in literature and the arts. In the course of time the original meanings of these words were deepened or expanded. Few of the terms developed by the court aristocrats of the Heian period (794–1185) in artistic criticism were ever intended for application to the bujutsu, but some were adopted by the warrior class at the time of its rise to power in the twelfth century. And by the Edo period many of these terms were being used by all citizens and had become part of the common heritage. The developers of the classical budo forms also adopted some of these special words.

Miyabi, the most inclusive aesthetic term, literally means "courtliness," or more freely, "refinement." The Heian court was a small isle of refinement and sophistication surrounded by a larger society marked by gross ignorance and coarseness. These court nobles, who were highly aware of and overly sensitive to their natural environment, looked with horror at the world around them. "Miyabi" was a term applied to their quiet pleasures, pleasures that could only be savored by those whose tastes had been "educated." Because miyabi represents the antithesis of simple virtues, the original use of the term led to a shunning of the rustic and of the cruder emotions. The term was used by the courtiers, in effect, to justify their sheltered way of life and express their contempt for the vulgar people surrounding them. This unrealistic attitude severely limited the range of early Japanese cultural expression among court nobles and was one reason that most of them cared little about the bujutsu.

The warrior, however, used the word "miyabi" in its broadest sense to include the elegance of his behavior, even his expert skill in the fighting arts. But other aesthetic terms are even more important to the martial disciplines. The poet Fujiwara Toshinari (or Shunzei), 1114–1204, in reference to poetry, advised the use of the "old" in the search for the "new," declaring: "We should seek to express emotions that our predecessors have not already described, but in so doing retain the language that they used." Another poet, Fujiwara Sadaie (or Teika), 1162–1241, not only echoed his ancestor but also established ten categories of beauty. It is *yugen,* one of Teika's "ten forms," that most directly applies to the classical budo. And, consciously or unconsciously, Edo-period citizens complied with the spirit of this Heian-period term as they felt the need for and sought to create incorruptible values in their artistic expressions. The classical budo is one such expression.

Yugen

The concept of yugen is profound and not easily defined. Teika's interpretation of yugen includes such ideas as "suggestiveness," "charm," and "dynamic stillness." Shotetsu (1381–1459), another poet, rejects "suggestiveness" on the grounds that it is a superficial quality much like that of the "aftersound" left in the mind as the sound of a ringing bell fades away. For Shotetsu, yugen must express the heart or soul of man as it permeates the object of his endeavor. But from any point of view, the essence of yugen lies in beauty and gentleness, the

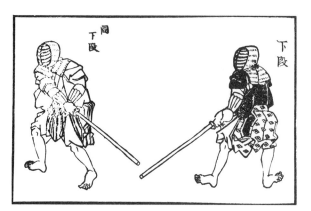 

tranquillity and elegance of a performance executed in a serene manner. Yugen also embraces the love of irregularity as seen in asymmetry used as a measure of perfection. Yugen is linked to Zen in respect to "no-mind" and to Taoist teachings in respect to "nonaction." Yugen can be comprehended by the mind but cannot be expressed in words, for its essence lies precisely in that "something" that is inexpressible. It can, however, be intuitively sensed as evincing the highest realm of artistic expression. Yet it is not enough to witness and learn about yugen from others; yugen is thoroughly understood only through one's own sustained efforts.

As applied to the classical budo systems, yugen relates to "mysterious skills," skills that a trainee acquires through direct experience and penetration of the hidden depths of spiritual discipline. The trainee is transformed within these depths themselves; he cannot be transformed through an external position in which he might seek to clarify the hidden. Yugen is intrinsically spiritual in nature. There is yugen, for example, in the sight of a master's technique, with its interplay of action and nonaction, for this reveals the spiritual strength of the master. Yugen thus relates to the power of expression, being a kind of internal symbolism in which vagueness—subtle suggestion rather than explicit statement—prevails. Perhaps the best approximation to a word express-

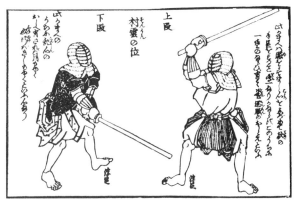

These woodcuts illustrate basic kamae, *or combative engagement postures, used in swordsmanship. Left to right:* gedan *(low position),* chudan *(middle position), and* jodan *(high position)* kamae, *and* gedan *versus* jodan. *(See also pages 56–57, 58–59.)*

ing the dominant elements of yugen is the English word "symbolism."

Yugen, in the classical budo, postulates a balance of visual and aural aspects of technique. The visual aspects, such as form, are, as signs or symbols, useful to show the relation of the concept of yugen—aesthetic ideal—to the classical budo.

Perhaps the most essential single element of physical form, as one aspect of the classical disciplines, is *kamae,* or combative engagement postures. Kamae are valuative in that they help the user to adopt the most appropriate behavior in a given situation. At the same time, they may be incitive signs, for if they are correctly interpreted by the viewer they become symbols that determine how the viewer must act. Custom and convention make some of the kamae arbitrary, though they may have natural foundations for their meanings; still, certain traditional elements are present to make them useful. The kamae were originally the warrior's behavioral semiotic: martial signs that symbolized certain attitudes and abilities connected with his profession. They were linked to the warrior's religious, intellectual, social, and artistic senses, and they constituted his range of technical knowledge of combat. But behind the physical form of the kamae lies a region only as deep as each viewer's technical knowledge can penetrate.

The meaning of any sign, such as a kamae, is determined by the habits it produces. The whole *raison d'être* of a sign, in the context of a warrior's behavior, is that it leads to or represents something else. The kamae, as a sign, has two meanings. Taken as an object (*signum specificative sumptum*), it has, like any real object, its own proper *esse,* which is directly present to the knowing power. But the sign as a symbol (*signum reduplicative sumptum*), besides representing itself, also represents something else. Kamae therefore have a direct, or manifestative, quality and an indirect, or significative, quality. In the widest sense, kamae are intelligible symbols based on physical form (stance, posture, demeanor, general physical attitude) by means of which warriors intuitively came to know something else: for example, whether the enemy was dominantly either aggressive or defensive, his state of confidence, as well as his degree of skill in combat.

A full grasp of the meaning of kamae must include an understanding of their relation to combat. In the case of the warrior and his bujutsu, the kamae were the spine of *satsujin no ken,* the "killing sword": that is, they were useful for menacing the enemy. Further, they prepared the warrior to meet the onslaught of his enemy. With his kamae the warrior sought to neutralize the chances for his enemy to gain the advantage over him. The classical budo, because they were essentially noncombative forms, deemphasized the bujutsu meanings of kamae, in some sense rendered the kamae combatively purposeless, and made of them little more than a visual representation of the spirit that activates the trainee.

The experimental method of training is common to both the classical bujutsu and the classical budo, for it is the natural way in which the human mind operates. Thomas Aquinas points out: "He who is drawn to something desirable does not desire to have it as a thought, but as a thing." For the classical warrior, during combat, a possible resolution of his problem would be suggested intuitively, and what was suggested was found to be worthy of retention in training when it yielded suitable results in combat. Classical budo disciplines, however, were formed in a less positivistic framework and show less influence of pragmatism on their technical structure. The refinement of the experimental method, as shown in the classical budo systems, is but an approximation of the older bujutsu methods. But it has a genuine originality of its own.

Through an analysis of the training methods of the classical budo, discussed in the following chapter, it is possible to understand better the differences between the bujutsu and the budo.

Kamae

CHAPTER FOUR

THE METHOD

There is, apparently,
no way open to mere human
beings to educate a man,
save by getting him to
educate himself.
                    Thomas Kane

The atmosphere of the classical bujutsu is that of Zen. To engage in such classical training is to learn the mode of Zen. It follows naturally that the characteristics of Zen must also permeate the classical budo forms; and those who do not appreciate Zen will not understand budo.

Intuition is the Zen method. For the classical warrior, kan, a kind of intuitive perception or intuitive penetration, was his "soul's gymnasium." Intuition carries with it a certain degree of what may be called "suggestiveness," something like the sound of a bell fading away after the physical act of ringing has stopped. But intuition goes deeper than this. It penetrates the very soul of one who relies upon it. Intuition brings to the classical budo forms a general simplicity that appears to have an unrefined aspect but which is not unrefined. If the method of intuition is deficient in articulateness, this lack is compensated for by the fact that intuition provides the key to long-term, psychological learning, which is dependent upon visual elements—copying actions—as opposed to short-term, logical learning, "the slow machinery of conceptual thought," which depends on sound—listening to or seeing words, those "noises on paper or in the air"—for its effect. What is known through short-term learning soon fades; that known by long-term learning is forever with the possessor.

Christmas Humphreys has aptly stated of intuition's role that "the intellect can toy with the concept; only the intuition can understand." Daisetz T. Suzuki has further amplified the significance of intuition: "Intuitionalism requires pointers more than ideas to express itself, and

Seishin

Kokoro

these pointers are enigmatic and non-rational. They are shy of intellectual interpretations. They have a decided aversion towards circumlocution. They are like flashes of lightning. While your eyes blink, they are gone."

The fullest activity of the mind is essential to the use of intuition. But nothing can be taught by the instructor or learned by the trainee unless the trainee applies himself with a desperate effort to the process of *seishin tanren,* "spiritual forging." What is given this effort by *seishin* (mind, spirit, soul), or "spiritual energy," is modulated by *kokoro* (mind, spirit, mentality), the "hot, sweat-bespattered core of man" that is the heart center of the creative power of the self. And because the classical budo forms are taught and learned from mind to mind and heart to heart, this is the most important point for a trainee to bear in mind: the workings of the mind and the sincerity of the heart categorically determine progress in pursuing the dō. Unless the trainee removes the staining influence of egotistical desires on his thoughts, and makes great demands on himself, he cannot succeed.

Through training one seeks affirmation, security, and contentment. Constant dedication to training changes the initially low intensity of the trainee's motivation into purposeful will, devoid of fear of failure, the desire to win or excel, self-pride, and the egotistical "I." A focusing and perseverance of will aims at the attainment of expert physical technique, but in the process the "I" is neutralized and fixed, allowing mastery to expose itself. Essential to this process is *hara,* described by Karlfried von Durckheim as "a mysteriously sustaining, ever renewing, ordering and forming power, as well as a liberating and integrating one." The quality of hara is a concomitant development of sufficient training and indicates the growth of an inner condition that affirms, in turn, that the trainee is making progress in self-cultivation. Hara is a state of mind that makes facing every circumstance a simple, unemotional matter. It enables the trainee to bear pain, discomfort, and adversity. Hara is the sure sign that the anxious, self-seeking "I" has been nullified. Its source of physical strength lies in the *tanden,* the "body's centerpoint," and manifests itself in the use of one's "middle." Without hara, physical form is lost, as is its unity with the self and the budo being studied.

Classical budo education is based on the concept of "self-activity." It is this activistic quality alone that guarantees learning. This is a creative kind of activity that seeks, discovers, realizes, and produces results. As the fundamental concept of learning, self-activity contains the idea that the trainee must establish a readiness for training. This means that he must feel a need for the training as something essential to his life. Entrance into a classical martial tradition, or *ryu,* recommends itself to a candidate for various reasons, but whatever the reason, there are three basic things that are required of him: 1) love for his chosen discipline, 2) a strong will to endure the rigors of discipline, and 3) an uncritical veneration for his master. In regard to the last, he should possess an obdurate devotion rather than what Eugen Herrigel calls "obtuse devotion." The candidate should also understand that he must subordinate all other things in his life to his dedication to training. A partial commitment to training accomplishes nothing.

Because nobody can pursue a dō without the guidance of a competent teacher, it is important for the candidate to seek out and be accepted by a true master, or meijin. This is not the simple matter it may appear. All rests on the ability to recognize a true master as distinct from an expert technician. To be accepted for training, the candidate must convince the master of his choice that he is of unusual strength of character; he will also need a formal introduction to the master made by somebody whom the master trusts implicitly. There is no substitute for a master. All else is, at best, a "translation" of how to set about classical training; the "original" lies in what is conducted by the master himself. Delaying the pursuit of a classical dō form until a master is found is preferable to self-tutoring or to training under one who is not a master.

There are certain levels of attainment that can be achieved before "enlightenment," the dō level, is reached.

The first of these is the *gyo,* or "training," stage. It affords the trainee an introduction to the *dojo,* the training area; the word means "a place for studying the way." The dojo is austere, a humble place of natural and quiet dignity. It may be a specially constructed, spacious hall or simply a small but suitable indoor area. Always cleanliness and order predominate. Inasmuch as the dojo links the spiritual and physical elements of classical budo, the basis of its construction must not conflict with that relationship. *Sabi* and *wabi*—naturalness, simplicity, rusticity (but not without an element of design)—are its keynote. Spirituality pervades the atmosphere of the dojo and is physically centered on the *shinden* (also called the *kamiza*), a particular area of the dojo where the

Gyo

Dojo

This unusual triptych of an Edo-period dojo depicts almost every form of classical budo, with both men and women shown training. Dojo officials are seated at the upper right. Among the weapons shown are the kusarigama, bo, *bow and arrow*, naginata, *sword*, shinai and fukuro shinai, *spear*, jutte, *and gun. Also seen are* jujutsu *and* horsemanship.

This woodblock print by Sakuragawa Horimasa shows kendo *training in a dojo under the aegis of Tokugawa bakufu instructors. The participants and audience are all samurai. A high official, perhaps the shogun himself, presides over the training session from a dais at left. Note that a fully standardized protective armor is being used by all trainees and that the* shinai, *or mock sword, is the only weapon permitted.*

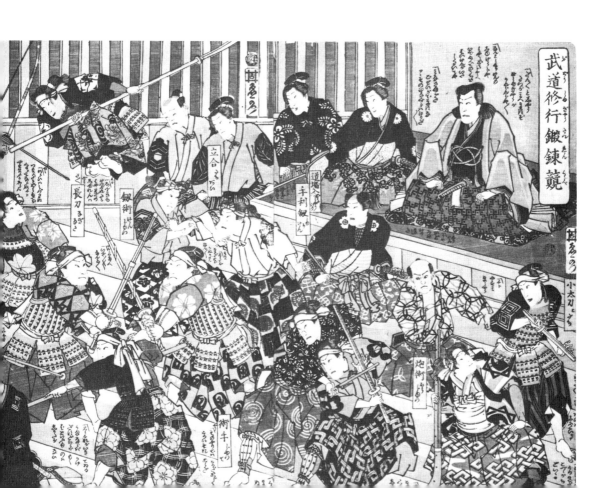

spirits, or *mitama,* of certain deities (*kami*) are enshrined. The trainee intuitively develops the right state of mind during training through the subtle influence of the shinden. It follows that the dojo must contain nothing ostentatious to distract the mind, for not only would this run contrary to the element of spirituality in the dojo, but it is patent that no really serious training can be pursued in a training area that contains all sorts of ornamentation.

The dojo is occupied by trainees at all levels of progress. The master has supreme authority, which he exercises through formal etiquette; the trainee is expected to conform to all such formalities, learning them by copying what he sees his seniors do. But to the inexperienced trainee, the dojo is nothing more than a place for physical exercise. Everything he sees, hears, or does stands outside his familiar, everyday existence. He is impatient with anything other than the actual physical action. But he quickly learns that the master requires "first things first." The long moments of silence, whether for meditation or as part of the technical training, are apt to be boring and painfully uncomfortable. He must sit in the traditional seiza position, a kneeling-sitting posture that brings his knees and ankles in contact with hard mats or a wooden floor. He is not allowed to stretch his legs or semirecline in search of a more comfortable position. The seiza posture is not purposeless, for it includes the beneficial effects of optimum safety for oneself and others, alertness, and economy of dojo space, and leads to flexibility and strengthening of the body. Hot during summer, cold during winter, the dojo has approximately the temperature of the environment beyond its walls.

In experiencing gyo, the trainee learns that the budo techniques must be practiced. He is on the "outside," a position of dense ignorance. Simply watching the performance of techniques by others, discussing them, or writing or reading about them is a mere circling around the technical perimeter of the budo. It is the master who is supreme in the life of the trainee at this stage, although sometimes inconspicuously so. The trainee must submit to the will of the master, who alone can guide the trainee to the dō. The trainee must be humble. He must exhibit *nyunan-shin,* or "soft-heartedness," a certain flexibility of spirit that attests to his readiness to accept things as they are presented by the master. The lack of this quality is indicative of pride and ego, the two elements of "mental stain" that attenuate learning and lead to mental friction between trainee and master. The master makes no apparent attempt to persuade or dissuade the trainee who lacks nyunan-shin but coldly continues his own training and supervising that of other trainees. But the resolute trainee does not quit; he follows his master.

The master knows when the trainee is in the right frame of mind to commence serious training. Such training, once initiated, begins and ends with the trainee in an attitude of intense alertness. Maintaining this alertness can be mentally exhausting. Training is a painful process of trial and error, of plodding with little explanation in a complex mire of technical difficulties. The master does not spare the trainee the burden of having to learn. He is overly critical of the trainee, calling attention to gross errors with a terrifying coldness. It is only the trainee's spirit of unbroken equanimity that allows him to accept this criticism in such a way as not to be afraid to meet more of it time and time again. But all this is part of a trainee's effort, or so the trainee thinks, and he is highly conscious of every mechanical detail of his own execution of technique. Great will and perseverance are needed by the trainee to carry him through the countless repetitions of basic movements. This is a time during which the nonessential is being eliminated and the essential brought to light. The trainee's questions are met by the master's laconic reply, "Don't ask, train." This is a time for "doing" by the key method of *kata,* or "prearranged form."

The kata method is of no real significance to the trainee, who invariably sees it only as something from which he cannot escape. In training he is apt to be overly conscious of his attempts to approximate the kata action. Much of it appears to be grossly unreal in relation to combat. The trainee is instructed to walk into the path of the weapon being wielded by his training partner, as though his doing so were nothing more than a casual matter not involving life and death, and then, at the last instant, to use his skill to avoid being struck by the weapon. But the dojo is a "death ground," a "field of life and death," literally the battlefield of life; the only difference between it and the battlefield of war is that in the dojo the trainee may die many times over and live to count these deaths as beneficial experiences toward learning his skills. These brushes with death occur at each training session; experienced over a period of many years they will lead the trainee to develop a balanced outlook on the matter of life and death—*seishi o choetsu,* literally, "transcending life and death."

Christmas Humphreys is right in his interpretation of the value of

Nyunan-shin

such training: "Death itself, when faced, accepted and, psychologically speaking, 'experienced,' has no more terrors, and this mental training explains the indifference to death of the Japanese samurai, whose military training included meditation as well as the physical arts of war."

The trainee regards any single kata as a confusion of technical parts. Its entire sequence appears to be an almost endless progression of movements in which the lapse of time between the different components is

exceedingly short; the trainee finds no time to think of what he must do or what comes next. The honest trainee knows nothing, can do nothing, and knows that he can do nothing; and he may be overwhelmed by the immensity of the task before him. Perhaps only the presence of the master convinces him to continue.

Silent communication is valued by the master, who often does not give the trainee verbal instruction. Uncomplicated directions are typical of his teaching. The master rarely speaks—he demonstrates. When verbal instruction is given, the trainee welcomes it but finds even then that often the master will contradict or retract earlier statements, saying, "Let me demonstrate what I mean; my lips have lied." The significance of this admission, which postulates technique as "truth in action," is never seen by the trainee, but his mind is being made aware of the fact that the master's method is superior to the analytical-verbal method.

The master "teaches" but avoids spoon-feeding his charges. The trainee is expected to ingest and digest the atmosphere created by the master, imitating the master's actions as best he can, and not to expect a blackboard lecture or presentation. Demonstration, example, and intuition bind the relationship of trainee and master, but too often the trainee sees the master as abrupt and authoritarian, as "no teacher at all." But the master lures the trainee with an unspoken thought, as in-

Spear training

timated in the words of Ananda Coomaraswamy: "Taste and see that it is good—for I know in what I have believed." All the master's instruction leans heavily toward symbolism, the value of which is a complete mystery to the trainee. Moreover, the trainee feels as if he is being compressed into a prepared mold. He suffers the feeling of a loss of self-expression as he slavishly copies what the master demonstrates. When he wishes to contest what the master makes him perform, he is tolerantly smiled at and put back on the track without there being any modification of the instruction. For the trainee this is a time of complete awareness of, and dependence on, mechanical copying of what he sees, repeated to the point of repletion. The trainee performs all his actions without knowing why he is doing them. An analogy with typing applies here. A person who begins typing does so in complete ignorance. He knows no touch-typing, knows that he does not know, and knows that he cannot type. All that he can do is follow the exercises given him, performing them awkwardly and with little accuracy. In the budo, this is the gyo level of development.

Training in gyo is a "blood, sweat, and tears" training and either makes or breaks the trainee. If accepted by the trainee, the rigid discipline begins almost instantly to remake him. The trainee then passes into what is known as the *shugyo,* or "austere training," level.

Unabated training is the method of shugyo, and the trainee experiences that discipline is the way to the dō. Conversely, by dissipation in easy living—an unplanned daily life— the trainee's energies are scattered and shugyo is made impossible. Shugyo requires the assiduous employment of self in order to discover the way to the dō. Shugyo is a process of "seeking a way out of a dilemma," a process that lies more in a spiritual application than in a mechanical one. The master deliberately places the trainee in technical dilemmas from which the trainee must escape by his own actions—for there is no other way out. Through the use of intuition the trainee can accelerate his escape, copying the only thing that is conveyable, the technique of the master.

Shugyo

But before the trainee can make good his escape he must invariably first drift around on a technical sea. The number of mechanical actions required of the trainee is, to him, overwhelming. This is largely because of his overreliance on his physical eyes in attempts to reproduce the actions of the master. And in his engrossment with the technical matters at hand, the trainee is very apt to mix the precise actions for one sequence of kata with those of another. He may even suffer "technical shipwreck." At any instant during training he may find that he has completely forgotten the order of the techniques; at times a whole kata sequence is "missing," and he is at a loss to know which one it is. But all these misfortunes are invaluable experiences for the trainee, for even in negative ways this experience urges the trainee to eliminate those courses of action that are incorrect. Should the trainee fail to recognize the course he follows as being incorrect, he will find his plight worsening until he flounders in the technical sea around him. Even then rarely does the master smooth the way for the trainee; usually the master allows the trainee's plight to reach a state of total hopelessness before tossing him a life jacket in the form of succinct advice.

The trainee voyages on. He is aware of a growing reliance on that "inner light," intuition, and with more receptivity than before the trainee accepts the master as a prototype and lets the master focus his mind's eye. At this stage of the trainee's development an unquestioning attitude toward the master is absolutely essential. He must also give full rein to the use of spiritual energy. The intensity of the trainee's seeking must be strengthened by the force of his spirit (kokoro). Without spiritual energy focused in this manner, no dō can be pursued. Through shugyo the trainee's spiritual energy is increased and the acuity of its focus improved. He thereby develops new strengths that are both physical and mental.

Technical problems confront the trainee at every training session. These require the direct application of a tremendous amount of physical energy. Particularly vexing is the problem of breath control, which must be performed, as Eugen Herrigel indicates, "consciously and with a conscientiousness that borders on the pedantic." Through proper breathing methods the trainee's whole body is strengthened, but what is more important is that the trainee's "inner self" obtains a hold on the spirit of the classical disciplines.

One aspect of breath control is the *ki-ai,* a term for which there is no adequate English equivalent. At the shugyo level of training the trainee's ki-ai resembles a kind of shout made by the forceful expulsion of pent-up air. The trainee must learn to make the ki-ai as if breathing "from the stomach" rather than from his lungs. A well-made ki-ai produces a characteristic sound that makes the ears ring; it seems to come from a source deep within the trainee and not merely to be caused by the vibration of his vocal cords. Though the intensity of the sound and the situation that produces it are quite different, the tonal fidelity of the ki-ai is much like the unforgettable, deep-seated rumble of a lion at bay. The ki-ai indicates the degree of integration of mind and body in the execution of a technique. It is an unfailing source of information for the master, who thereby knows the trainee's level of achievement.

Ki-ai

In overcoming technical adversities the trainee begins to recognize "truth in action" and to understand it. "Truth" is not yet his, but he is moving toward it. The consuming effort by which he engages in shugyo, and which has led to the immersion of his self in voluntary discipline, is reshaping his life. The trainee's patience with small details will one day gain for him mastery of larger things, but for the present it makes him acutely aware of the intricacy of the accumulated experience of centuries. As he executes his techniques the beauty of method and spirit, as combined in physical actions, is slowly revealed to him; he stands in awe as he considers the creative genius who formulated the discipline he now shares with his master, his fellow trainees, and those who came before him.

In shugyo, as in gyo, repetition is the core training method. Exemplified in kata, these exercises serve to reinforce the lesson that motor skills are not to be learned by words but through action. Kata are filled, as it were, with physical *koan,* or conundrums, situations that evoke technical crises. They are devices through which the trainee's mind is shocked into action. Physical koan are to be met head on and conquered in the sense that they are overcome through adherence to prescribed form; and even when this is not achieved, a degree of controlled skill is developed. Whether skill develops poorly or not is of little consequence, for it is the quality of endeavor, endeavor made without artifice and with a sincere heart, that matters. Through meeting and solving the physical koan it is suggested that what is learned is comprehended not by analytic thought but by a unity of will and dedicated effort. Kata now becomes the expression of the trainee's mind and body, a mirror that reflects the degree of their integration. Kata brings the trainee to realize that his mind and body have been going in divergent directions to a considerable degree, as evidence of which the mind often calls for the performance of a movement by the muscles that the latter fail to carry out.

The physical koan provide the master with opportunities to give valuable object lessons to the trainee. The master may deliver a knock or blow to the trainee, and the trainee may often lose some blood. It is not uncommon for the master to reveal in this way the weakest points of the trainee's technique. When the trainee grips his weapon wrongly, for example, he may be given a sharp, stinging blow on the knuckles, sometimes hard enough to remove skin. When he is not protecting himself correctly by his posture or movement, the master may deliver a hard blow to the exposed area, leaving a welt on the trainee's skin. Or, to teach alertness to a laggard, the master may attack the trainee without warning and hurl him to the ground. Unpleasant as these object lessons may be, the trainee is saved from being discouraged by the apparent callousness of the master through understanding that there is not the slightest personal malice behind it. Still another physical koan is frequently used by the master to "awaken" the trainee. The master uses

Koan

sound or silence at moments when the trainee's action is sterile. The master engages the trainee as his training partner in kata and emits a resonant ki-ai at a chosen moment in their performance. The sound of the master's ki-ai is ear-piercing, and acts as a stimulant to the lethargic trainee; the trainee feels as if he has been mentally struck by his master. The ki-ai also combines and binds the trainee's energies. Conversely, the trainee who has grown accustomed to the master's ki-ai at certain moments within a kata is shocked when the master omits that electrifying sound; he hears only layers of silence that deafen him.

The trainee often finds himself making excuses for his technical deficiencies. He is overly conscious of the "I" in what he does; this consciousness pushes his spirit (kokoro) backward. He is indulging in self-deception, a mental crutch that is an absolute obstacle to learning. It must quickly be set aside if progress toward the dō is to continue. The trainee's demonstration of self-deception does not in the least affect the master, who continues to order and set the proper personal example in training. Therewith, the master may choose deliberately but subtly to make a mistake in his technique, then happily apologize to the trainee for his "lack of skill." The alert trainee takes his master's "confession" to heart. Other important transformations take place in the trainee's outlook. The dojo becomes respected as a place of severe confrontation between oneself and one's self. What was previously simply a structure in which to be trained now becomes quite personal and plays an important part in the daily life of the trainee. The complexity of formal dojo etiquette is now a part of the trainee's memory. The occasional quick correction dropped into the silence of the dojo from the mouth of the master, this combination of almost wordless teaching and silence, can make a firm impression on the trainee, who heretofore has regarded the master's teaching as "no teaching."

The typing analogy can be applied to the shugyo level. Dedicated effort in touch-typing drills consisting of the repetition of fundamentals brings the learner to a point of minimal familiarity with the keyboard. He can now begin to find some of the keys without constantly looking at them, though only by a strong conscious mechanical awareness of what he is doing. Errors fill his drills. He knows of typing and can type a bit but is not yet a typist in the strict sense of the word.

Shugyosha

The budo trainee, now a *shugyosha,* or "austere exponent," travels on, broadening his skills and acquiring new ones. After certain rudimentary actions become conditioned reflexes, the trainee reaches beyond mechanical movement to awareness. He now realizes that he can correct technical deficiencies only by continuous training. At this point the trainee's motivation is strong enough to bind him forever to his study and pursuit of enlightenment, the dō. Quitting or turning back is impossible now. He has entered the *jutsu,* or "art," stage of development.

At the beginning of the jutsu level of attainment the trainee is rarely satisfied with his skills. He feels an "unfinishedness" in his technique and is acutely aware of the need for pursuing technical perfection. By continuing to train he feels that he is closing the gap between his present skill and that of his master. Yet there is a certain amount of uneasiness and frustration experienced at this stage. In his striving, the trainee realizes that he is just short of technical perfection; a lingering awareness of the dependence upon mechanical movement shows up this deficiency, though it grows less apparent as he progresses. A sense of "limitedness" overtakes him, for he is powerless to accelerate the pace of his technical progress. In spite of this, technical skills are becoming a natural expression for him. He has experienced "truth in action" and is on the path to becoming the master of his physical actions, though not yet of himself.

The trainee at the jutsu level becomes more concerned with the possible combative significance in his techniques than with the idea that they are to be used for noncombative purposes with a finished artistic form; any disjunction between combative reality and the form required of him by the master disturbs him. But he journeys on, confident in his master's injunction: "Why try to anticipate in thought what only experience in action can teach?"

At this level the trainee sometimes develops an air of idle self-gratification that gets him stuck in his achievement as confirmed by successes and magnified by renown. The master foresees this and heads the trainee off before it is too late. Without the master the trainee would at this point fall into the bottomless pit of vanity. The master humbles the trainee by engaging him personally in kata training and pointing directly, through such action, at the trainee's limitations. The trainee is chagrined to find that at times he completely forgets what he is to do; his mind is a complete blank and techniques cease to come naturally. At other times, conscious of his own limitations, the trainee tries desperately to avoid technical error, especially in the presence of his master, but fails miserably because he is thinking too much about what is to be

Using fukuro shinai

done. The master tolerantly and laconically indicates the need for "more training."

The spirit of kata, heretofore a burden to the trainee, is now understood, and its practical essence is seen with the "eyes of the mind." In the fluctuation between the symmetry and asymmetry of its component parts, kata suggests completeness, and the trainee now realizes that this is so. He understands that kata composed of a balance of fundamentals—stances and postures, movements, and manipulations of weapons—made to both right and left are symmetrical in nature; kata that require the user to make these same actions only to one side or the other are asymmetrical in nature. Neither kind of kata can, by itself, be used to train a man to control his mind and body fully under any and all circumstances.

The "answers" to the physical koan are to be found within the trainee, and the master serves only as a guide who enables the trainee to work out the necessary solutions. The method of kata is always repetition, both mechanical and spiritual. The mechanical aspect leads to technical mastery, yet stands in the way of spiritual mastery—mastery of the self. It teaches only how to achieve technical skills. Those who would follow only the physical aspects of kata miss the principle behind the art they perform. They are too busy with technique to see beyond it. Mastery of self can never be theirs unless they accept and pursue the spirit of kata. Without spiritual growth no trainee can progress beyond technical skills, which are only acts of cleverness. Mastery of self as a goal requires the trainee to achieve liberation of spirit by an "inward-turning" in which all artificialities and mechanical aspects give way to a spontaneous functioning of the self. Even in mastery of jutsu, when there seems to be nothing more to be learned in a technical sense, the sensitive trainee finds the feeling of incompleteness always with him. The "unquietness" is his unconscious self trying to move into consciousness. An inner calm is necessary before that becomes possible, and that inner calm requires the trainee's further maturation.

The kata, which once seemed very long, now appear to be so short that often the trainee feels he has left out some portion. The intervals that lie between the component parts—those moments of no action—once consumed in a flash of time now appear to lengthen to the point where the trainee finds that he has "time on his hands." This is because technique has become integrated with the trainee's self, a state of tech-

A jujutsu tactic

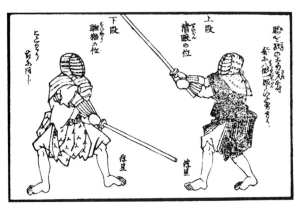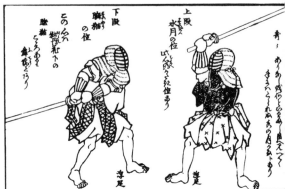

Shown in these woodcuts are various combinations of kamae. *Left to right:*
gedan *versus* jodan, gedan *versus* jodan, chudan *versus* jodan, *and* chudan
versus jodan. *(See also pages 38–39, 58–59.)*

nical mastery that allows him to view the overall technique as technically simple.

The degree of integration is easily discovered by the master, who
uses a physical koan to test it. During the performance of a kata, the
master, acting as the trainee's training partner, will, prior to completion
of the kata, deliberately stop his own actions, leaving the trainee
"stranded" in the midst of a technical crisis. The sudden "absence" of
the master shocks the trainee, who then reacts in one of two ways. If he
continues his movements after the master has stopped his, the trainee is
acting mechanically; he is merely running a scale of exercises that he
knows quite well from his past experience. Should the trainee, however,
stop simultaneously with the master, it indicates that the trainee is making full use of his spirit. In the former case, the master knows that the
trainee's spiritual development is not yet sufficient and that they train
only as independent and spiritually isolated individuals. In the latter
instance the master is satisfied that both he and the trainee train together
as a whole.

The instruction given by the master continues to be an exercise in intuition, not in rational argument, just as it has been throughout the earlier stages of gyo and shugyo. But if before the jutsu level was attained
the trainee had received encouragement from the master, however
slight, now there is none. The master requires the strictest attention to
detail and allows no mediocrity. Often he will backtrack, taking what
the trainee had assumed to be already learned, and will give it new and

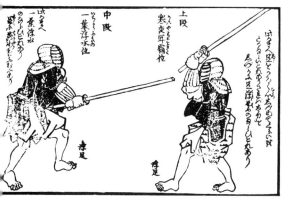

fuller meanings by emphasizing aspects the trainee has never considered. The trainee realizes that his skill was developed by training and must now be maintained by even harder training. Each session with his master is precious. It is *ichi-go ichi-e,* "one period, one encounter," each session an opportunity to share a training experience with his master that comes only once.

So close has the relationship between the trainee and his master become that they understand each other even in complete silence. This is because the trainee's mind has been trained to attain approximately the quality of his master's mind, sensitive and perceptive to the slightest inner workings of the master. But there is a touch of sadness at this stage of the trainee's development. From the outset of their relationship the question of how far the trainee would travel in his quest for the dō has not been the concern of the master, for he knows that someday the trainee must go on alone. It is only now, at the jutsu stage, that the trainee himself realizes this. He is exhorted by the master to "climb on the shoulders of the master" and surpass him.

There can be no slackening of the trainee's efforts now. He must adhere to the discipline that has brought him this far and intensify his efforts, for without these he cannot be assured of the fruits of his labor. Technical training must be the focus of all his energy. The kata must be performed until confidence that he will perform them correctly is reached. These performances must exhibit qualities beyond the purely mechanical. The master will occasionally test the trainee by unexpect-

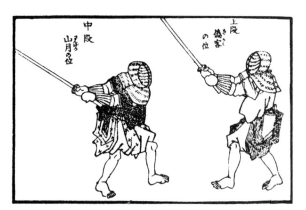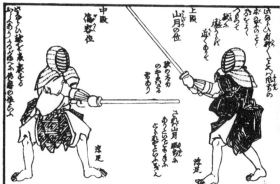

These kamae *show, left to right:* chudan *versus* jodan, chudan *versus* jodan, *and* jodan *versus* jodan. *(See also pages 38–39, 56–57.)*

edly announcing a change in the order of the separate kata. As the trainee expects to have to execute a particular kata, the master deliberately moves to yet another. The jutsu-level trainee of sufficient experience can instantly adapt himself to this physical koan and solve it in the appropriate manner. Failure to do so is evidence that more rigorous training is neccessary.

Suddenly skill is there, no longer needing thought. The trainee has confidence that he can repeat kata without error, and he is now a master technician; it is a refreshing experience. Technique mastery is first accomplished in the jutsu stage, but though the master technician controls his skill admirably, he does not yet fully control himself. Dō is still absent.

The typing analogy applies equally well to the jutsu level. Though the person typing depends less upon his mechanical awareness of the keyboard, errors are still possible. The required keys can be struck with reasonable accuracy and speed, bringing some efficiency into his typing. He is a typist, knows typing well, and can type, but he is still without the polish of mastery. The keyboard positions can be named without difficulty, but they cannot yet be physically manipulated with identical perfection. The typist realizes that in spite of technical mastery he does not yet possess self-perfection.

Not until the state of "artless art" has been reached can the master technician claim to be master both of his art and of himself. This level is the ultimate, the dō, the equivalent of Zen enlightenment, or satori,

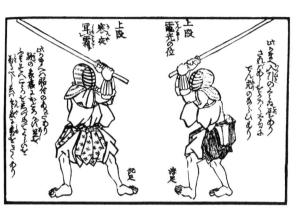

"self-realization." The dō is the gyo-shugyo-jutsu levels brought to flower. Attainment of the dō represents, beyond mere perfection of motor skills, a self-perfection in which old habits of dependence upon mechanics are thrown away and restrictive thought, or awareness of "I" or "I am doing," is lost. It is the stage of the accomplished, the true master, which is characterized by a maximum of mental poise, alertness, and spiritual and emotional control. At this stage physical technique, or "truth in action," has been mastered, transcended, and forgotten in that there is now no need for an awareness of mechanical actions. The master of the master technician is no longer able to recognize whether it is mind or hand that produces the technician's technique. The mind has been trained to focus sharply and is now one made "pure" by the removal of the "stain" of the ego. This "pure" mind is *makoto*, the "stainless mind," which is undisturbed by external nonessentials. The vehicle for "truth in action," the dō, is also forgotten, and the master technician, as a master of himself, is now himself "truth in action." This attainment can be recognized by outsiders (people who are totally uninvolved with the classical disciplines) as being a supernormal achievement, but it is not possible for them to realize it from their outside position. Even the most educated mind fails to understand dō unless it has experienced it, for in the words of Dante: "Who paints a figure, if he cannot be it, he cannot draw it."

Makoto

The new master sees kata for the first time in their entirety. William Blake wrote: "The cistern contains; the fountain overflows." Kata, as

Warrior preparing for archery practice

A jujutsu *throw*

the fountain, is filled with an unending vitality. And within the genius of any master lies the ability to design new kata that are both meaningful and lasting. Such attempts by less skilled persons are but meaningless efforts of self-deception.

The typing analogy will again serve to illustrate. After sufficient experience in typing, the typist becomes a master touch-typist. He no longer needs to depend upon the mechanics of how to type, nor has to rely on memory to find the positions of the keys. He makes few errors if any, and has the speed and accuracy that give his typing the mark of the master. He know typing, can type, and knows he can type: he is a master typist. Though he is a master he readily fails one test that a less trained typist can usually manage with ease. This is the keyboard recall test. The master cannot quickly recite the keyboard from memory, for he has forgotten the locations of the letters. But in spite of his "forgetting" we cannot truthfully say that he cannot type, nor that he is not a master typist.

Classical budo training involves much more than can be explained in terms of externals. An inner process of development is taking place in the trainee. This development matures only through protracted training. The inner work is more important than the outer accomplishment because it will outlast the external action. When accomplished it will endure because it stands perfected. Practice brings the trainee to the realization that he can be seized by the insight of his training (intuition acting in the unconscious), and that the mastery inherent in him all the

Woman with kusarigama   *Test-cutting with a sword*

time can now be liberated. Whoever aspires unweariedly can come to realize what his practice will bring. Although by systematic, unwavering dedication to training he can be guided by a true master along the "way" that will make him a master also, mastery itself is never transmitted from one person to another; it is not a "shoving in" process. It comes from within one's self; it is a "leading out" process. The master's task is only to illuminate technique by illustrating it; the trainee must realize it himself. To do so he applies intuitive penetration (kan), which allows him to use the master's enlightened state as a model. He does this through practice.

By "practice" and "mastery" the Japanese warrior understood certain very specific things. One can "practice" only when one has acquired and mastered technique. Before this one is merely assembling building blocks, and he can only be said to be "training." Only the whole can be "practiced." Thus, true practice begins only at the jutsu level, the stage of development at which outward form has been mastered. It is at this stage that the real work begins—that of molding and finalizing the self. In classical budo training the aim of practice is not the visible, physical results but the inner development gained through experience and insight. This was postulated by Confucius in *The Doctrine of the Mean:* "In the archer there is a resemblance to the gentleman. When he misses the mark, he turns and seeks the reason for his failure in himself."

Mastery, for the warrior, is that level of attainment which guarantees

Zazen

the perfect result. Genuine mastery in physical skill presupposes a certain degree of inner quality—that is, a highly trained unconscious. Conversely, training for a skill can lead to inner self-mastery as well as outward mastery of a technical skill. Thus, it is not what "comes out" in a physical sense but what "goes in" and "comes out" in a spiritual sense that is important. If the trainee understands this, he understands a great deal and does not question it when he is told that it is not important to hit the target with a weapon when practicing classical budo forms. He readily sees that practice of a skill serves an ulterior purpose, the development of the self.

For the warrior, experience came first in his training; gradually an insight into what the training was doing for him was realized; and finally, the trainee became free to practice. Experience and insight, as gained from training, which entails repeating actions over and over again, always precedes actual practice, and the order of experience and insight is never reversed. Every action repeated possesses the potentiality of inner perfection. Training that is persistently carried out leads to real ability, and only real ability can produce the perfect result, which is self-mastery. The Zen master Okada Torajiro gives the following analogy: "Keep a carp in a pond with a stone in the center, and another carp of equal size in another pool which has nothing in the center. In the pond where the stone is, the carp swims around the stone all the time, and thus has its exercise based on energetic turning actions. It grows more quickly than the carp in the other pond. This is the result of endless repetition."

By experience and insight one comes to understand the purpose and limits of practice, but prior to attainment of the dō level the trainee may develop undesirable qualities of self. All trainees must be aware of these and adjust themselves accordingly.

One symptom, a desire for "backward turning" sometimes manifested at the gyo level, is due to one's ego working in the face of failures. The discouraged trainee finds it easy to stop striving and may stop training altogether. Another symptom that occurs below the jutsu level is that of "false crediting," the error of giving oneself total credit for any progress made. Training is carried on by personal willpower, but it is through the guidance of the master that the trainee moves ahead. The master assists discovery by and within the trainee.

The symptom of "spilling" is common to trainees of shugyo level.

Here the trainee may habitually speak of his training experiences, not realizing that this leads to the destruction of technical soundness already attained and the prevention of new technical growth. Inner growth also suffers, for it does not thrive on talk. Strength comes from the damming up of experience, not from spilling it. Yet another symptom is that of "standing still" in the face of progress. This is most likely to happen at the jutsu level. It is fatal to further achievement. Immediate success must be knocked out of the trainee's hands by new, hard tasks. Here is where the master is essential. He must keep the trainee blind with his own intensity of purpose to train properly; merely reeling off practice like rote learning or a dance is an off-track approach. The trainee must be made to realize that the goal cannot be aimed at technically. The warrior saying, *"Katte, kabuto o o-shime yo!"*—"After victory tighten your helmet cords"—shows his anticipation of harder tasks yet to come, and it is well that the trainee make this his motto.

Zen permeates and invigorates all stages of a trainee's development. Zen is addressed to the individual and is like a finger pointed at the trainee's mind. At first (gyo) he can only see the hand; later (shugyo) he sees the finger; still later (jutsu) he sees that the finger is pointing; and finally (dō) he sees what the finger is pointing at.

The classical warrior immersed himself in Zen meditation, *zazen,* to gain self-confidence. His efforts furnished him with a calm acceptance of fate. He developed the quiet submission to the inevitable and the stoic composure in the face of danger that Nitobe Inazo appropriately called "friendliness with death." The fully trained warrior transcended thoughts of life and death (seishi o choetsu). The founders of the classical budo systems adapted many of the techniques of the classical bujutsu in order to underline the reality of death as an aspect of life, not necessarily centered on the consequences of combat. Nevertheless, the kata of the classical budo are filled with situations that are "flirts with danger" or "flirts with death." Deliberate movements bring the trainee to a razor's-edge nearness to his weapon or the weapon of his training partner.

In the dojo, where classical budo training is conducted, meditation, called *mokuso,* is practiced in the seiza position. This is an exercise in which all trainees sit in silence for brief periods, usually after the completion of the day's training. The trainee does not simply "sit in forgetfulness" but sits rather to develop presence of mind. Meditation gives a chance for the vital "loosening" of one's inner powers. It is a practice

Mokuso

that builds hara, that patient, calm, and undisturbed coolness of mind essential to classical disciplines. Meditation is a catalyst to wisdom; wisdom is the function of meditation. Through meditation the trainee brings himself to a new dimension in spiritual strength, literally a new frame of mind. The strength so gained is elastic and durable, for his frame of mind brings an inner awareness enabling him to respond to whatever situation may arise.

Zen makes much of the "everyday mind" of the Chinese Zen master Ma Tzu (Buso; d. 788). As soon as we reflect, deliberate, and conceptualize, the original unconsciousness is lost and a thought interferes. Calculation is miscalculation and is detrimental to the warrior. Zen instilled purposelessness in the warrior and in the classical budo training methods. At the gyo level the trainee has no technical knowledge. He moves in a clumsy way, but the innocence of his untutored state permits him some degree of freedom of mind. In the shugyo stage the trainee moves mechanically, as if "pushed" by thought; he has little freedom of mind. In the shugyo stage the trainee's mind is often "stopped" at technical junctures when he most needs fluidity of action; the result is gaps in his execution of a technique, which demonstrates that he has only intermittent freedom of mind. At the jutsu level the trainee finds that his mind, which was "hardened" or "localized" in the earlier levels of attainment, has now become almost completely free, and he is able to move and meet situations demanding quick response. At the dō level, as a master, he realizes complete freedom from technical barriers.

Zen

Daisetz T. Suzuki touches on these phenomena in his discussion of the "immovable intelligence," the constituent of all masters of the budo forms, noting that the novice trainee parries a blow aimed at him, doing so in ignorance and without thought or need to think; there is no stoppage of his reaction because the unconscious is untrained and operates instinctively. But as the trainee develops more skill he thinks and thereby slows his action-reaction process. A blow aimed at this trainee often is not parried, as response to it becomes caught in the "crush of intellection." But as the trainee develops still more skill and becomes a master himself, he ceases to think and again reacts with "ignorance." Suzuki thus identifies three levels of skill: 1) an untutored level of ignorance at the start of training (gyo); 2) the area of shaded "half-knowledge," where reactions are dimmed by thought (shugyo); and 3) the jutsu and dō levels, where skill is once more ignorance, but ignorance produced at the end of intelligence. And only the final level permits sure results.

Purposelessness, as developed by Zen methods designed for the warrior, does not entail the absence of things or thoughts, nor is it simply nothingness. It is a state of mental balance that is characterized by "no harboring." Harboring drains mental energy. Harboring the idea of a foe goes against the fundamental principle of all Japanese classical martial disciplines. When a grain of sand gets in one's eye, the eye cannot remain open—it closes reflexively. Similarly, a confused mind turns against itself and is its own enemy. Training, including meditation, enabled the warrior to dismiss harboring. Bokuden writes: "When the foe-form ceases to exist, you are not conscious of it, nor can it be said that you are altogether unconscious of it. Your mind is cleansed of all thought movements and you act only when there is a prompting from the unconscious." Bokuden is suggesting that spiritual skill, the working of the "trained" unconscious, is the concentration of all the physical and psychical forces, which enables the master to dispose of controlling or reflecting intelligence. This is *myo-yu,* a compound term built from *myo,* "something beyond the bounds of analytical understanding," and *yu,* "movement" or "operation," in which deliberation has no role. Suzuki explains it thus: "The act is so direct and immediate that intellection finds no room here to insert itself and to cut it to pieces." It is the achiever's mastery of his self, mastery of the dō, that creates myo-yu in him.

Musha-shugyo

One Zen custom used by the classical warrior and adopted by the exponents of the classical budo forms is *musha-shugyo,* a kind of "austere training in warriorship." Musha-shugyo requires the trainee to travel in monklike fashion, living simply and exposing himself to natural hardships in the course of travel. At the same time this voluntary pattern of life involves him in training sessions in as many different dojo as he can enter. Musha-shugyo is indispensable to the trainee at the jutsu level of skill and is a path of rugged endeavor that is a prerequisite for mastery of the dō. Most of the founders and developers of the classical budo ryu engaged in musha-shugyo, and by testing and proving their techniques, as well as their own mastery, through this activity were able to formalize the component systems of their ryu. The creation and functioning of many hundreds of these ryu played an important role in the history of Tokugawa Japan. We will examine a few of the major ryu in some detail in the following chapters.

CHAPTER FIVE

THE FORMATION OF THE BUDO SYSTEMS

A good system is twice blessed—
it blesses him that trains
and him that's trained.
Herbert Spencer

On the whole, the first half of the seventeenth century was well suited for the initial development of the classical budo systems. Under the Tokugawa administration Japan was enjoying a time of high culture, but a culture that was on the verge of decay. It culminated in the Genroku era (1688–1704), during which citizens developed high standards of taste in literature and the arts. In the highly compartmentalized social structure of Tokugawa society, social prestige was all-important; therefore it was only natural that the members of the four social classes—*shi* (warriors), *no* (farmers), *ko* (artisans), and *sho* (merchants)—should have sought every means to attain social influence.

By the mid-seventeenth century, martial heroes were being replaced in popular favor by devotees of etiquette, of the arts, and of letters. Martial strategy and tactics became academic issues, and the systems of the classical bujutsu were regarded for the most part as historical curiosities. Instead of surpassing the level of combative autogeneity achieved by the classical warriors prior to the Edo period in their development of weapons and fighting arts, the Edo-period warriors began to classify and overorganize what remained of the martial profession.

These warriors, having neither to fight nor to toil, became combatively ineffective and socially nonproductive. Some of them became actors, connoisseurs, artists, or poets. In general, the elements of a stern and frugal life, so essential to the professional warrior's vitality, were absent. Most of the Edo warriors were a thriftless lot, and it was inevitable that the rapid expansion of the nation's economy would diminish the importance of their social class; for the very economic process that served to enrich the lives of the commoners raised the cost of living, to the disadvantage of the warriors. This was but one sign of the growing importance of the commoners.

Though Tokugawa Japan lolled in a state of comparative peace there were forces at work that made the bakufu uneasy. How to keep the martial efficiency and morale of its warriors at an optimum level in an age of peace was recognized as the major problem for the bakufu leaders; at the same time, an excess of martial ardor might easily upset the delicate balance of society as tared by the docility of the warrior class. Also vexing to the bakufu was the problem of control over the ambitious daimyo in the provinces. These influential men controlled highly autonomous feudal domains called han, and in spite of legislation by the bakufu to curb martial buildups in the han, the spirit of the classical warrior and efficiency in bujutsu flourished there. Apparently the bakufu also believed, with Cicero, that "farmers make the bravest heroes," for in 1661 it issued orders prohibiting farmers from having firearms. In 1668 it forbade merchants and traders to wear swords.

The changeover from the use of the sword as a primary weapon of combat to its use as an instrument solely for training mind and body in the pursuit of the perfection of individual character was conditioned by the circumstances of Tokugawa society. But there was another strong though less immediate influence that also aided the changeover. The disaster that had befallen the classical warriors of Takeda Katsuyori in 1575 in the battle of Nagashino at the hands of Oda Nobunaga was still fresh in the minds of the early Edo-period warriors. The complete slaughter of the gallant classical warriors at the hands of commoner conscript soldiers bearing firearms signaled to many alert minds the diminishing value of the sword as a weapon of war. Yet the sword was specifically chosen over other weapons to be the leading instrument in a new role in the classical budo. This was not solely because the sword had been the central weapon of the classical warrior—his "living soul"—but because the sword was also one of the divine objects of

Oda Nobunaga

This Kunisada print of a Kabuki scene depicts two warriors fighting in kenjutsu *fashion. It is fairly true to life except that the right-hand figure should not have a finger on the swordguard.*

the imperial family (the *Sanshu no Shinki,* or "Three Sacred Regalia," comprising sword, mirror, and jewel) and, as such, was inseparable from the Japanese national ethos.

Classical budo ryu, *perse,* first appeared at the time of the transformation of *kenjutsu* (sword art) into *kendo* (sword way) in the first half of the seventeenth century. The essence of kendo was stated at that time to be more a spiritual discipline for the improvement of personal character than an activity directly concerned with combat. The stress on nonmartial aspects was not entirely new, as will be seen, but this was the first time that swordsmanship in any form had been openly offered as available to all classes of people. Thus the conversion of kenjutsu to kendo, in a social sense, stood as a heretical development within the strictly segregated Tokugawa society. Other classical bujutsu ryu, as well as

A woodblock print by Hokusai shows two men practicing swordsmanship with
bokken, *or hardwood swords. Each man is trying to force the other off balance.*

still others founded in the Edo period, followed the lead of the changeover from swordsmanship considered solely in its practical battlefield
aspects to swordsmanship as a spiritual discipline. All of them idealized
the reflected past glories of the martial profession, but in so doing
bypassed the significant martial implications of the previous periods.
The bakufu did nothing to interfere with the development of kendo,
seeing it as being no more than quasi martial in character, and a discipline that might well be useful in channeling the energy of its citizens
into desirable endeavors.

In surveying the development and nature of the component systems
of the classical budo it is useful to divide those systems into two major
categories: systems based on weapons and "weaponless" systems. We
shall consider these categories in some detail in the next two chapters.

CHAPTER SIX

CLASSICAL WEAPONS SYSTEMS

And sheathed their swords
for lack of argument.
Shakespeare

FROM KENJUTSU TO KENDO   Swordsmanship—kenjutsu—in the pre-
Edo periods was specifically an art of aggression. In spite of its very practical nature, however, there were warriors who devoted themselves to
a thorough study of this art, probing beneath its technical aspects to
great philosophical depths. Many of these warriors found that the practice of kenjutsu instilled in them a sense of inner peace and an outlook
on life that made them abhor the killing of fellow human beings. Such
feelings are fundamental for the naming of the art of swordsmanship as
a vehicle of the dō, or "way."

The Tenshin Shoden Katori Shinto Ryu is Japan's oldest historically
proven martial tradition. The *makimono* (hand-scrolls) that record the
teachings of this ryu contain a clear emphasis on the ethical conduct of
swordsmen. Kenjutsu, an art developed to defeat enemies, is not to be
indiscriminately used. This sense of moral awareness is intrinsic in the
teachings of the founder of the ryu, Izasa Ienao (1386–1488). Ienao
was appointed an instructor in kenjutsu to Yoshimasa, the ninth Ashikaga shogun (1435–90), but retired soon after his appointment to avoid
involving his ryu in the malpractices of Yoshimasa's bakufu. Yoshimasa had sanctioned Ienao's teachings, but the high-principled Ienao
refused to accept this recognition, entered a Buddhist order, and retired from public life. Changing his name to Choiisai Ienao, he continued his martial study at the Kashima and Katori shrines (in present

Ibaraki and Chiba prefectures, respectively), traditional centers of buju-tsu study. There he brought his teachings to a high intellectual level and influenced a great many swordsmen, of whom Tsukahara Bokuden (1490–1571) was perhaps the deepest and most introspective thinker.

Bokuden studied kenjutsu with his father, a Shinto priest at Kashima Shrine, with his father-in-law, and with many of the famous kenshi who resided in the area of the Katori and Kashima shrines. Bokuden's skill grew to prodigious heights, and as a kenshi he is alleged to have been undefeated in thirty-nine combats. But Bokuden was overtaken by the spirit of self-reflection and developed over the years what he referred to as the "mutekatsu ryu," a kind of swordsmanship in which no hands are needed. The following well-known anecdote reveals the nature of this development.

One day as Bokuden was crossing Lake Biwa in a small boat crowded with passengers, a swordsman was boasting of his unmatchable skill with the sword. His loud manner caught the attention of all the passengers and the oarsman. Only Bokuden, apparently asleep, was ignoring him. The braggart, disturbed that anyone should fail to learn of his skill, shook Bokuden rudely from sleep and defiantly asked what ryu of swordsmanship Bokuden followed. Bokuden replied: "The mutekatsu ryu."

"What's that?" asked the swordsman. Thereupon Bokuden explained that this style of swordsmanship was the highest form of skill possible with the sword, for it relied on the use of no hands. Bokuden's answer made the swordsman angry. He shouted: "You mean that you can defeat me without using your hands?" Bokuden replied quietly in the affirmative.

"But why then do you carry two swords?" asked the braggart swordsman, growing still angrier.

"I use my swords only to vanquish my own selfish desires," answered Bokuden. The swordsman, now fully enraged, ordered the oarsman to head for the nearest land, where he might engage Bokuden to settle the issue. But Bokuden voiced concern for the lives of innocent people who might happen to wander into the combat and suggested, instead, that they go to a small island nearby. The swordsman agreed. As the small boat was beached on the island the impatient swordsman leaped ashore, threw off his cloak, and stood ready for combat. Bokuden rose slowly from his seat, removed his jacket, and to all eyes appeared about to follow his challenger ashore. To the great surprise of all, especially the boastful swordsman on the beach, Bokuden then quickly picked up an oar and shoved the boat out into the lake. As the stranded swordsman bellowed with rage, Bokuden called out to him in a calm but clear voice: "This is how the mutekatsu ryu defeats the enemy."

Bokuden's "mutekatsu ryu" is based on a principle that has a much deeper meaning than is indicated by the humorous incident alleged to have happened on Lake Biwa. It is a principle based on original thought that is traditionally credited to Bokuden, though it is possible that he was conditioned by the thinking of other kenshi at the Kashima and Katori shrines, in particular those of the Katori Shinto Ryu and Kashima Shinto Ryu. Though the "mutekatsu" principle is manifested in swordsmanship, its essence is that of Zen and traceable only to the teachings of the Zen master Takuan (1573–1645), who stated: "Some think that striking [with the sword] is to strike. But striking is not to strike, nor is killing to kill." Takuan was closely linked with the swordsmen who gathered at the Katori and Kashima shrines in the seventeenth century. His philosophical teachings affected the greatest swordsmen in his and succeeding ages. His philosophical discourses had an especially penetrating and lasting effect on the later development of the Shinkage Ryu.

Kamiizumi Ise no Kami Fujiwara no Hidetsuna, also known as Kamiizumi Musashi no Kami Fujiwara no Nobutsuna (1508–78), founded the Shinkage Ryu in the first half of the sixteenth century. Japan was at that time in the throes of the *sengoku jidai,* the "age of wars." The sword was the law of the land. As a disciple of both the Tenshin Shoden Katori Shinto Ryu and the Kage Ryu, Kamiizumi Ise no Kami trained assiduously and proved himself a masterful technician in combat, such as he engaged in during musha-shugyo. This led him to improve on the teachings of the Kage Ryu and to establish his own martial tradition, the Shinkage Ryu. In his search for a worthy successor, Kamiizumi Ise no Kami engaged Yagyu Tajima no Kami Taira no Munetoshi (1527–1606) in combat, defeating the latter by using the *kiki-hada,* a sword made of bamboo strips covered with the skins of toads; this mock weapon allowed combat without the danger of serious injuries. In 1566, Kamiizumi Ise no Kami passed on the secret principles (*okuden*) of the Shinkage Ryu to Yagyu Tajima no Kami, who was also a former disciple of the Tenshin Shoden Katori Shinto Ryu, and thereby acknowl-

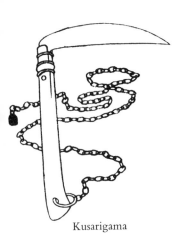

Kusarigama

edged Tajima no Kami as the second headmaster of the Shinkage Ryu.

Yagyu Tajima no Kami served in 1571 as kenjutsu instructor to the sixteenth and last Ashikaga shogun, Yoshiaki (1537–97). The Shinkage Ryu functioned during a time of violent social disturbances. Not only was the shogun a mere puppet in the hands of administrators who controlled him, but the bakufu was no longer a martial organ. At this time new social classes arose, and powerful social forces emerged from the interaction of 1) the emancipated agricultural workers; 2) the wealthy merchants, traders, and moneylenders; 3) the *ji-samurai* (farmer-warriors), who, growing in strength, organized associations to hamper the bakufu's rural-area officials, whose job it was to administer the land and its revenues; and 4) the ambitious buke that were in the process of seizing national and provincial governmental offices.

In this distracting environment the Shinkage Ryu was brought to technical perfection. Kenjutsu was still useful in its primary role, that of a method of combat. After the last Ashikaga shogun was deposed in 1573, Yagyu Tajima no Kami went into retirement. He refused the request of Tokugawa Ieyasu, in 1594, to be an instructor of *hyodo* (martial methods) in Mikawa (present Aichi Prefecture), perhaps because he did not want to become an instrument in the hands of the political forces that were contending for the leadership of the country. Yagyu Tajima no Kami's fifth son, Yagyu Matazaemon Munenori (1571–1646), however, accepted a position as instructor in hyodo to the second Tokugawa shogun, Hidetada, and his teachings, including kenjutsu, became the basis of the Edo Yagyu line, as distinct from the Bishu Yagyu line, of the Shinkage Ryu.

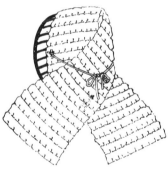

Early men *seen from rear*

The great social changes taking place in Japan during the Edo period affected the course of the Shinkage Ryu, but these changes were only the catalysts by which the philosophical essence of the ryu became better developed and defined. The name Shinkage Ryu can be written with two entirely different sets of ideograms. One set points simply to the proper name of the tradition; the other, to the spiritual awakening of that tradition. All teachings of the Shinkage Ryu have a decided philosophical flavor, and the methodology is that of Zen. Although skill with the sword is to be acquired and maintained on a level of combat efficiency, this skill is to be exercised without deliberate effort or purposeful mind. It is to be used *munen,* with "no reflection," and *muso,* with "no thought." This is a state of mind in which the technique is "perfect

Master swordsman Ozawa Takeshi of the Hokushin Itto Ryu receives a cut by kenshi *Ozawa Kiyoko, his wife, on his* kote *during a* kumi-tachi *training session.*

Sasamori Junzo, almost ninety, headmaster of the Ono-ha Itto Ryu, assumes a typical Itto Ryu kamae, *the* hongaku no kamae, *against another swordsman.*

emptiness, yet therein something moves and follows its own course" as a natural act of the consciousness free from conceptualization and deliberation.

The method of oral transmission from master to disciple is used to convey the innermost secrets of the Shinkage Ryu. These secrets may not be divulged to the uninitiated, but it is permissible here to indicate them by making use of the exact line of verse that the masters of the Shinkage Ryu use to summarize their secret teachings. That verse, "The waters of the West River," is similar to the one uttered by the Zen master Ma Tzu in answer to a query from one of his disciples. A plethora of complex metaphysical concepts is embodied in this Shinkage Ryu verse.

One concept is the working of the "original mind" (a Zen term, later used by Neo-Confucians of the Wang Yang-ming school) based on intuition, that is, "good knowledge" (knowing right to be right, wrong to be wrong, without deliberation), which culminates in "great-perfect-mirror wisdom" (the Wang Yang-ming idea of an "inner light of the mind" that precipitates "illustrious virtue"). For the kenshi of the Shinkage Ryu, the sword is the principle instrument for vanquishing one's

Otsubo Shiho, Zen priest and a master teacher of the Edo Yagyu Shinkage Ryu, takes the gyaku no kamae *using a* bokken.

Two disciples of the Maniwa Nen Ryu engage in spirited kempo *training using* fukuro shinai *and the heavily padded helmets and* kote *typical of this ryu.*

selfish desires. Through shugyo, a process of spiritual cultivation that becomes "noncultivation," the kenshi develops *mushin,* a state of "no-mind." The headmaster of the Shinkage Ryu awards each of his master swordsmen a curious special certificate in recognition of technical skill and moral merit. On the certificate is brushed, in black ink, the simple figure of a circle. The empty circle symbolizes the "emptiness" and "no-mind" of the kenshi.

Another of the pre-Edo period martial traditions, the Maniwa Nen Ryu, featured a singularly effective type of kenjutsu, which it called *kempo,* "sword method." By the late seventeenth century, however, the Maniwa Nen Ryu had adapted itself to the peaceful tempo of Tokugawa society and exhibited the softening effects of civilian social ethics. In its dojo the following injunctions were posted:

1. Kempo is an art of self-preservation.
2. Kempo must lead to the preservation of human life, not the taking of life.
3. Kempo is an art that consists in *wa* (peace), not in defeating an enemy.

The fine distinction between swordsmanship as an art primarily concerned with "self-protection" and the principle of "not defeating an enemy" was thereby acknowledged.

Ito Kagehisa (1560–1653) was a warrior renowned for his superlative skill in swordsmanship. For him the exemplar of swordsmanship lay in the use of one sword technique only. He evolved a theory which stated that an infinite number of techniques could be derived from a single basic sword technique; he named that single technique *kiri-otoshi* (cutting down). On the basis of his theory he renamed himself Ittosai, "one-sword-[technique] man," and founded the Itto (one-sword-[technique]) Ryu. Ittosai's practical experience in combat urged him to probe metaphysical realms; for in the process of developing thoughts that transcend life and death (seishi o choetsu), Ittosai faced the severest combat of his career—that against his own ego—and fought to overcome the double anxiety that must inevitably accompany thoughts about having to live or having to die. He concluded that all things in the world have a common origin and similar end, though each undergoes different processes in the role that it plays on earth.

Ittosai's brand of swordsmanship influenced such great men as the sixteenth-century warlord Oda Nobunaga, as well as both the second

*Takano Kosei (right), head-
master of the Nakanishi-ha Itto
Ryu, engages an instructor of the
ryu in* kenjutsu.

and third Tokugawa shogun, Hidetada and Iemitsu, and must therefore
be included in any serious investigation of the forces behind the change
from kenjutsu to kendo.

The main purpose for which a warrior must study swordsmanship
was, for Ittosai, not to acquire an effective technique for combat. A person with unsound moral values would only destroy himself should he
persist in gaining skill in the use of the sword for combat. Ittosai's teachings suited the Tokugawa bakufu's scheme of things, for they fitted in
admirably with that government's administrative machinery. Ittosai
taught that warriors who hoped to master swordsmanship must be
versed in both the literary and the martial arts, bun and bu respectively.
Bun and bu were to be regarded as the two sides of the same thing, as
inseparable for the proper functioning of man as are the two wings of a
bird if it is to fly.

Because Ittosai reflected on swordsmanship as developed in an age of
warriors by warriors and for warriors, and because the sword was the
incarnation of the classical warriors' spirit, he believed that swordsmanship should remain the privilege of warriors. It must remain closely related to the ethics of the warrior's profession and be the basis on which
the warrior strives to lead an ethical and virtuous life, he taught.

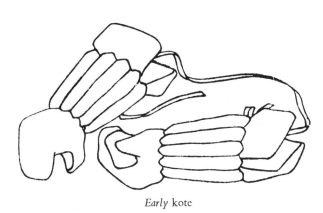

Early kote

This triptych by Kuniteru Yosai shows a late Edo-period kendo bout being held in a sumo wrestling ring. The referee, also in the ring, is a sumo wrestler. Seated at right is the judge.

Master swordsman Shiokawa Terunari (black kimono) of the Mugai Ryu engages instructor Kasegai Takashi in tachi-uchi swordsmanship.

The teachings of the Itto Ryu urged the warrior to attain a "higher" personality, that is, one that was more suitable to a peaceful society. This was to be achieved through cultivation of the ability to act with complete moral integrity in everyday life. There are three attributes that the Itto Ryu requires of its exponents; these are referred to in the expression *shin-ki-ryoku*. *Shin,* or mind, enables the self to determine what is right and good from what is wrong and evil. *Ki,* or spirit, is the inner power by which one carries out that which is judged to be good and therefore right even at the risk of losing one's life. *Ryoku,* or energy, is the physical power through which one manifests and practices good and right.

Ittosai disliked the term "kenjutsu," which for him signified nothing more than a crude martial art. He chose, instead, to call his kind of swordsmanship *heiho*—Itto Ryu heiho. Ittosai explained the reason for his choice by stating that kenjutsu was an art of killing, while heiho was an art of protection. Though killing and protection may be but two aspects of the same thing, for the art of protection often has recourse to killing, and vice-versa, Ittosai declared that the difference lies in the priority, or stressing, of one element over the other.

The famed kenshi Miyamoto Musashi (1584?–1645), of the Nitten-ichi Ryu, famous for his skill with two swords (*nito*), extended the meaning of heiho. Musashi, in his *Gorin no Sho* (Book of Five Circles), states that "heiho must be lined with morals." Morals cannot be developed if swordsmanship is pursued only with the idea of mastery of technique, the terminal level of kenjutsu; a swordsman must address himself to "higher values," that is, spiritual values.

During the Edo period, in spite of some dissension over the choice of the term "heiho" as a substitute for the word "kenjutsu," heiho became the usual term used when speaking of swordsmanship. This word epitomizes the changes that came over kenjutsu during the Edo period.

Itto Ryu heiho aimed at *katsujin no ken,* that is, taking advantage of the movements of the adversary. This secret principle of the Itto Ryu posits that the highest level of swordsmanship is that of keeping the sword in its scabbard—of not having to draw one's sword in order to prevail. Ittosai reasoned that it is a normal human desire to want to be the victor in any endeavor. The Itto Ryu psychology and its application in technique exploit this natural tendency of man. Kenshi of the Itto Ryu deliberately put themselves in positions seemingly of disadvantage,

Fukuro shinai

apparently inviting the enemy to strike them. Showing neither fear of losing nor desire to defeat the enemy, the Itto Ryu kenshi believes that his mind is free from evil intentions and thus capable of reflecting perfectly the enemy's thoughts and actions. This is an extension of the classical warrior's concept of *makoto,* "stainless mind."

Though the teachings of the Itto Ryu do not stress killing, they retain a practical flavor by which balance is restored to what might otherwise be only speculative philosophy. Nothing is to be found in the makimono of the ryu that says that the enemy is not to be killed. In fact it is abundantly clear from an examination of these scrolls that when acting in accord with right and good the kenshi may be required to draw his blade. But it is also stipulated that the kenshi has the obligation first to try sincerely to gain an overwhelming psychological advantage over his adversary by keeping his sword in its sheath. This is the key to the "highest victory," much as with Tsukahara Bokuden's "mutekatsu." In this sense Ittosai's heiho is the equivalent of the use of suspended judgment in daily living; it exemplifies the use of reason through nonhostile actions in an honest attempt to contribute to peaceful living. For a man to be able to act according to such high standards, Ittosai points out, he must first know himself thoroughly through austere discipline, then must act on the basis of awareness of heiho. Ittosai's moral point of view in regard to swordsmanship rests fully on moral courage. Another of its aspects is courtesy. Courtesy to others must be developed beyond superficial decorum. Only when the virtue of courtesy reaches a substantial depth is it truly a virtue and one that allows a man's own "mental government" to be natural.

Abe Gorodaiyu (fl. 1668) is the first man known to have used the word *kendo*. Kendo, or *ken no michi,* "the way of the sword," describes the teachings of his ryu, the Abe Ryu. Gorodaiyu, a disciple of the Taisha Ryu, devised a method of swordsmanship in which the emphasis was on mental and moral training rather than on just gaining expertise in a physical technique. At about the same time, the Heijo Muteki Ryu, founded by Yamanouchi Renshinsai, also used the term "kendo" to describe its teachings.

Thus the philosophical undertones of the pre-Edo martial traditions were amplified and became overtones in the ryu created during Edo times. Philosophical concepts exerted a softening influence on the practical idea of effectiveness in combat and took swordsmanship out of its

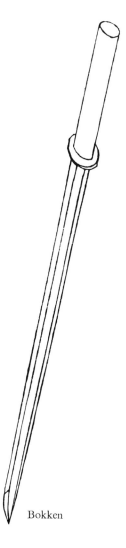

Bokken

predominantly combative role, making it more a spiritual discipline. Swordsmanship as kendo spread among all social classes and became an attitude toward life and a way of thinking for many of its participants.

In order that kendo might become fully acceptable in a peaceful society it was necessary to devise some means by which training could be carried out with a reasonable degree of safety. Heretofore, in kenjutsu, swordsmen had used live blades. This had proved to be not only a dangerous but also a costly practice; swords inevitably suffered damage, requiring that they be repolished, if not entirely replaced. Nor was the *bokken,* the hardwood sword, less dangerous in training. It was natural, then, that concern to avoid injuries should have encouraged swordsmen to devise ways by which trainees could be protected. Their efforts brought about far-reaching effects on Japanese swordsmanship.

The modification of the sword for training purposes began in pre-Edo times. Both the Maniwa Nen Ryu and the Shinkage Ryu, as well as the Yagyu Shinkage Ryu, found it expedient to substitute a *fukuro shinai* (a mock sword made of bamboo encased in leather or heavy cloth) for the live blade or bokken. But the most significant contributions toward improving the practical margin of safety in swordsmanship must be credited to Nakanishi Chuta (fl. 1750).

Chuta learned his swordsmanship as a follower of the teachings of Ono Tadaaki (1565–1628), the founder of the Ono-ha Itto Ryu, which was formalized in the latter half of the seventeenth century. Ono Tadaaki, a disciple of Ittosai, had devised a mock sword for training purposes. Nakanishi Chuta eventually left his master out of deference to him; for Chuta's skill exceeded that of his master. Chuta quickly organized his own tradition, which he called the Nakanishi-ha Itto Ryu.

Chuta's brand of swordsmanship was clearly of a kendo nature. The techniques of the Nakanishi-ha Itto Ryu relied heavily upon attacks made against the wrist of the training partner, so Chuta devised protective gloves, the *kote*. Because he was dissatisfied with the clumsy *shinai*

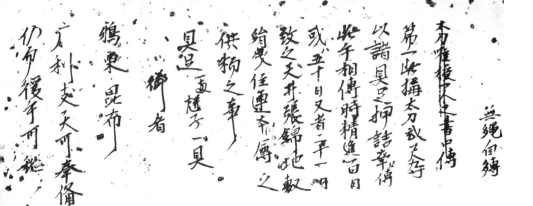

This is part of a hand-scroll attributed to Izasa Choiisai Ienao, founder of the Tenshin Shoden Katori Shinto Ryu, on kenjutsu techniques.

(mock sword) that had been designed by his former master, Chuta refashioned it, giving it greater balance. He encased strips of bamboo in a heavy cloth cover and attempted to make the weight of this new mock sword approximate that of a real sword.

The use of protective gloves and the new mock sword were not immediately popular with all trainees. Furthermore, the insistence on certain rules that guided the conduct of all trainees in his dojo caused many swordsmen to leave Chuta and seek other masters. But there were those among the trainees who saw an advantage in being able to strike with the mock weapon against specified areas of the training partner's body without having the slightest fear of doing injury.

In the last quarter of the eighteenth century, Chuta increased safety in kendo training. He designed a trunk protector, called *do,* to be used with the kote and the improved shinai. The shinai was made lighter by standardizing its length and making it from only four strips of balanced and seasoned bamboo; a leather *tsuba* (handguard) was added.

The growing popularity of kendo brought about a variety of other modifications that cannot be credited precisely to any one person. With the improvement of protective equipment and the addition of such pieces as the *tare,* or groin protector, and the *men,* or mask, as well as the development of a standard training costume, the *ken dogu* (equipment for kendo) was complete. And even before the nineteenth century, commonly accepted rules governed trainees with regard to prohibited matters, such as deliberately striking unprotected body areas, and methods of evaluating individual technique.

During the nineteenth century kendo, despite opposition, became popular among commoners. So widespread was its practice that the rules governing its methods were standardized, and its already only quasi-martial nature was diluted still further by the confinement of its techniques to prescribed postures and actions. The progress of trainees could be compared by having them compete safely against one another and by scoring their strikes, thrusts, and other technical matters. Thus

Swordsman versus spearman

it was that the original basis of kendo as a spiritual discipline—a classical budo form—veered into a new direction and increasingly took on the character of a sport.

A late-Edo martial tradition called the Hokushin Itto Ryu illustrates the trend toward compromising between kendo as a spiritual discipline and kendo as a competition between pairs. Chiba Shusaku (1794–1855) founded this ryu and called its style of swordsmanship *kumi-tachi*. Shusaku, a commoner, allegedly developed his style of swordsmanship to satisfy his desire for social prestige. The essence of Shusaku's swordsmanship was fully in accord with the classical budo to the extent that he had made it a spiritual discipline. But he went beyond considering swordsmanship as an individual discipline and brought a distinctly competitive flavor to its practice. Shusaku, himself a master swordsman, was big and powerful, two factors that made him eminently successful in encounters with other swordsmen of his time. Though he could and did use his superior physical strength to good advantage, Shusaku nevertheless insisted that the soul of swordsmanship rests in excellent technique, not in crude physical force. Four points underlay his teachings:

1) Silence: move any time, any place, in any efficient manner, but without making noise.
2) Walk: take whatever number of steps the situation requires, but do so in a natural manner.
3) Use the *uchi-kote* (also called *oni-kode*), protective gloves, in developing cutting ability.
4) Use a bokken that is straight—one with no *sori,* or curvature.

Shusaku and his kenshi of the Hokushin Itto Ryu emphasized competitive exercise. Spirited bouts were an essential feature of Shusaku's training methodology. He and his successors also encouraged competition between kendoists and exponents of the *naginata* (short-bladed, long-shafted halberd); a lightweight mock weapon made of wood was used to simulate the real naginata. Some of the bouts featured male kendoists pitted against women armed with the mock naginata, and these bouts were the focus of great attention and popularity among townsfolk, who paid admission to see such attractions.

In spite of the high degree of feudal decentralization that was achieved in the late Edo period, there were signs of rising nationalism. This would be brought to a head still later in the period, when local rivalries were

A woman of samurai lineage trains with a bokken.

subordinated in an effort to meet the challenge of the intruding West-erners. And in the Meiji (1868–1912), Taisho (1912–26), and Showa (1926–present) eras there would be temporary distortions of kendo as a classical spiritual discipline for the purpose of bolstering that nation-alism. But these developments lie beyond the scope of this book.

FROM IAI-JUTSU TO IAI-DO   The designation of "sword-drawing tech-nique" as a distinct budo form, *iai-do,* was made only in the twentieth century. But the essence of iai-do, a noncombative discipline engaged in for the individual's spiritual cultivation, is clearly a product of Edo-period thought.

Iai-jutsu, the classical sword-drawing art practiced for combative pur-poses, was contained in the curricula of hundreds of martial traditions that existed prior to the Edo period. For the kenshi who specialized in iai-jutsu, the sword was to be drawn quickly and struck accurately into the target. During the peaceful Edo period some of the ryu that featured iai-jutsu died out, but the majority continued to function, while new ones emerged. The socially privileged Edo-period warriors continued to wear the *daisho* combination of long and short sword, and as long as the sword served as the symbol of the warrior class, there were those warriors who saw a use beyond the practical for sword-drawing tech-niques. These visionaries were responsible for employing the sword as a spiritual instrument, using it in a manner distinctly different from that of iai-jutsu; these men were the pioneers of the disciplines that are today called iai-do.

Orthodox tradition claims the original essence of iai-do to be the product of the genius of Hojo Jinsuke Shigenobu, more popularly known as Hayashizaki (or Rinzaki) Jinsuke. There are all sorts of ideas as to the details of his life, but most of them are pure fiction. In the twentieth century, in order to bring prestige to iai-do, Jinsuke's name has been accorded a high place of honor among devotees of this budo form.

Only a few facts are definitely known about Hayashizaki Jinsuke. He was born in Sagami (present Kanagawa Prefecture) in the mid-sixteenth century. That he had combat experience is unproven, but the *Bujutsu Taihaku Seiden,* an Edo-period manual, states that he spent seven years, from 1595 to 1601, studying swordsmanship. He then devised a system of sword-drawing techniques that he called *batto-jutsu,* a term equivalent

A young member of an Edo-period gang strikes a defiant kamae.

Master swordsman Omura Tadaji of the Muso Shinden Ryu assumes the tate-hiza posture (left) prior to drawing his sword in iai-do fashion. At right he is shown completing the nukitsuke, or draw. (These photos and the photo of Omura Tadaji on page 34 are by Quintin T. G. Chambers.)

to "iai-jutsu," and gave his style the name Junpaku Den. To test himself and to establish his teachings, Jinsuke toured various provinces in musha-shugyo fashion. He gathered many disciples. When he was seventy-three years of age (around 1616) he toured for the second time and then disappeared; no one ever heard of him again. Hayashizaki Jinsuke's influence on swordsmen was great; during the Edo period more than two hundred ryu primarily concerned with sword-drawing techniques emerged, stimulated by his teachings.

The successors to Hayashizaki Jinsuke embodied their teachings under the name Shin Muso Hayashizaki Ryu, generally subsumed today in the Muso Shinden Ryu. Jinsuke's successors can be traced with certainty through the eleventh headmaster. Thereafter a split in the ryu developed, and one segment terminated with the teachings of Nakayama (Hyakudo) Hiromichi, the sixteenth headmaster; the other segment claims continuity in its teachings down to the present, and nineteenth, headmaster, Kono Momonori. Modern exponents of the Muso Shinden Ryu generally regard the line that ended with Nakayama Hiromichi as the true centerline of the ryu.

All the evidence indicates that Hayashizaki Jinsuke may have taught

Left: Takenouchi Tadao, headmaster of the Takenouchi Ryu, demonstrates iai-jutsu-*style sword-drawing with the* kodachi, *a specialty of this ryu. Right: an Edo-period depiction of* iai *technique (a detail of the triptych on pages 44–45).*

only a kind of "quick-draw" technique. His choice of the word "batto" (literally, "striking sword") to describe the sword in action affords a clue, for the term "batto" includes the implied meaning "to strike instantly" with the sword. Thus, Jinsuke's method differed little from the older systems of iai-jutsu, many of which also used the term "batto-jutsu." It also appears that Jinsuke may have taught that his system of drawing the sword was to be used only in a limited way during combat, that is, only as a defensive art useful in meeting the attack of an assailant. If this is so, his method differed from the older iai-jutsu systems, which were both offensive and defensive systems as the situation demanded.

In the hands of Hayashizaki Jinsuke's successors the Muso Shinden Ryu underwent both technical and philosophical changes to a degree that greatly reduced its original combat effectiveness. These changes are further evidence of the social forces working in the daily lives of Edo-period citizens. These forces were reshaping the role of the warrior in that society, and in fact were challenging his very special social position. With this, the Edo-period warrior was reduced to being a warrior in little more than name.

Two of the technical characteristics of the Muso Shinden Ryu method

of sword-drawing indicate that its exponents introduced combatively inane mannerisms. The first of these characteristics shows that the Muso Shinden Ryu teachings included techniques of drawing the sword that were not suited to the battlefield. Seiza, a starting posture for many of the techniques of the ryu, was, for the classical bushi of pre-Edo times, a position from which he rarely expected to draw his sword. From the point of view of attacking, seiza is a "dead" posture, as is *tate-hiza,* in which the swordsman sits on his left foot, which is tucked under his buttocks, and raises his right knee. The pre-Edo warrior much preferred iai-goshi, a low-crouching posture in which his right knee was raised; this kept him off damp or soiled surfaces and afforded him instant mobility and great speed in drawing his sword to meet an emergency. But seiza is well-suited to an urban, peaceful way of life, and in the Edo period the warrior, as well as other citizens, frequently used that posture. Thus Hayashizaki Jinsuke's original teachings led to the establishment of the *zashiki* (seated etiquette) sword-drawing technique, the product of a peaceful age.

Related to the seiza posture is the second of the technical characteristics of the Muso Shinden Ryu that indicate that its teachings were primarily intended as a spiritual discipline rather than as an effective combative form. All exponents of this ryu disregard the fact that even the Edo-period warriors, serving in peacetime, wore the daisho. When seated, the manner of wearing the sword in the Muso Shinden Ryu requires that the *odachi* (long sword) be positioned in the sash with the cutting edge upward, so that the tsuba, or handguard, is in front of the centerline of the body at the height of the navel; the normal manner of inserting the *kodachi* (short sword) in the same sash, also cutting edge upward, is thus made impossible. Even if it is considered that the odachi had been removed, as was required of warriors when entering or occupying certain structures, the Muso Shinden Ryu is curious, for it does not train the exponent in the use of his kodachi; in reality, even when the odachi was removed a warrior always retained his kodachi.

In the standing posture adopted by exponents of this ryu, again only the odachi is worn; this too does not conform to the warriors' custom of wearing the daisho. But even if this breach of custom is admitted, the position of the odachi, when the wearer assumes a standing posture, quickly leads to an unpardonable breach of etiquette. Because the wearer's scabbard (*saya*) juts abruptly outward behind him at his left side it

Right: this delightful print shows Edo-period boys engaged in kendo training ▷
in a dojo. The two pairs of contestants wear standardized protective armor
and use shinai. Lower left and lower right: these prints depict Edo-period
gang members during battles between rival gangs.

90 WEAPONS
SYSTEMS

will inevitably cause *saya-ate*, the knocking of the scabbard against some
person or object as the swordsman moves. Inadvertently committed
saya-ate was a dangerous breach of etiquette and was to be scrupulously
avoided. For when saya-ate occurred, the warrior's code of ethics regarded it as an insult answerable by recourse to the blade. Even before
the sound of the saya-ate died away the offended man might draw his
sword and cut down the offender from the rear. In the fully combative
tactics of the Shinkage Ryu (Bishu Yagyu) the technique called "saya-
ate" was a deliberate act that provided the swordsman with the calculated chance to be "insulted" and to cut down his "offender" with a
swift and well-directed stroke of the sword.

These and still other technical weaknesses, from the point of view of
combat, appear in many of the ryu founded during the Edo period.
They are in some measure due to the martial ineptitude of the Edo-
period warriors, and also to the great influx of commoners who participated in sword-drawing techniques but knew nothing of the technical
aspects of wearing and using the daisho. Thus, whatever the original
sword-drawing techniques of Hayashizaki Jinsuke may have been, over
the course of years the teachings of the Muso Shinden Ryu and many
other ryu became truly only spiritual disciplines. The Muso Shinden
Ryu summarizes this kind of discipline as "the attainment of a way
through which to cultivate a tranquil mind that will serve the possessor
under all circumstances." The Muso Shinden Ryu teaches one to have
no enemy in mind when training and to discipline oneself daily so that
a new level of mental acuity can be achieved. Spiritual training is first
and foremost; this is followed by training for general improvement of
the body. The teachings of this ryu are an exemplary classical budo
discipline and serve to indicate clearly the differences that separate a
jutsu form from a dō form.

Another splendid example of the use of the technique of sword-
drawing primarily as a spiritual discipline is found in the Mugai Ryu.
Behind its dynamic style of aggressive swordsmanship called *tachi-uchi*,
which appears to the casual eye to be no different in purpose from that
of the purely combatively oriented methods of swordsmanship, lies a
spiritual essence that is exemplary of the classical budo forms. The personal background of Tsuji Getten Sakemochi (1650–1729), who
founded the Mugai Ryu in 1695, indicates in what way this essence
came to develop.

The headmaster of the Kashima Shinto Ryu, Yoshikawa Koichiro (left), engages a master swordsman of the ryu in kenjutsu *using* bokken.

Tsuji, the son of a farmer, began his experience with swordsmanship as a disciple of Yamaguchi Ryu kenjutsu when only thirteen years old. Later, as a master swordsman in the Yamaguchi style, he established a dojo in Edo in 1676 and attracted a large number of disciples, both bushi and commoner. In keeping with the spirit of his age, Tsuji took a great interest in the Chinese classics; he also participated in Zen meditative disciplines. In short, the Mugai Ryu was the product of Tsuji's more than thirty years of constant austere training, which led to his "enlightenment."

The main purpose of the teachings of the Mugai Ryu is the execution of moral doctrines determined in accordance with right reason. Tsuji regarded his teachings as being defined by an expression composed of two ideograms: *hei,* but pronounced *hyo,* which means "military"; and *dō,* "way." Thus the term *hyodo* signifies the absorption of the military spirit within the framework of right reason. Tsuji further made it plain that the essence of hyodo was an aspect of the original Chinese meanings for *yin* (*in* in Japanese) and *yang* (*yo* in Japanese). The former refers to a negative principle, evidenced in the absence of light (shadow), while the latter implies a positive principle, evidenced in the presence

In this Edo-period kendo *bout depicted by Hokusai both com-batants wear* men *and* kote. *Seated at right is a* dojo *official.*

of light (brightness). According to Chinese philosophy, yin and yang represent cosmic principles or forces always present in phenomena and always interacting.

Tsuji's methods of sword-drawing were guided by this principle of the interaction of yin and yang. He maintained that civil and military spheres of human endeavor are but manifestations of yin and yang. Each depends on the other, and they are inseparable. For him the act of founding and maintaining a state represents civil virtue; the process of governing it, military virtue. In connection with the latter, Tsuji writes: "The art of using a sword is a great source of power in governing a state, for it represents simultaneously an instrument by which to subdue internal and external enemies of the state."

Tsuji also sought to balance practical martial effect with civil order (the "sword of justice," used when necessary to maintain law and order and social harmony) in his methods of drawing the sword, a compromise which if ignored, he believed, would confine sword-drawing techniques to the jutsu level. Tsuji emphasized that Mugai Ryu hyodo was not intended to be a method of killing but was concerned with the cultivation of the swordsman's spirit. Hyodo aims at the unification of academic accomplishment (literary arts) and combative effect; it further suggests loyalty to his country as the inescapable duty of every good citizen.

The idea of using a sword for self-protection is played down in the Mugai Ryu. Tsuji taught his swordsmen to calm their minds through discipline, to hold no image of an enemy in their minds. He noted: "People who have a great interest in martial arts [bujutsu] ensure domestic peace. In my own case I have devoted myself to swordsmanship ever since my childhood. Through training, including [Zen] meditation, I approach life with a calm mind. My heart [spirit] and hands are united into one. . . . I know that the art of swordsmanship [hyodo], which teaches us how to cope with an enemy, holds value for everyday life. When you reach sufficient training and progress in it you will see no enemy, that is to say, you will 'go into' the enemy's heart. There you will reach an altruistic and matchless state. You are then the unification of being and naught."

During Tsuji's lifetime there were signs of corrupt practices among the exponents of the classical budo forms. Crass exhibitionism, in which the conservative and sober values of the classical disciplines were blatantly ignored, was indulged in. Some exponents turned to using their skills to earn money by entertaining an audience that had paid a small admission fee to see something sensational. In full awareness of these and other malpractices against the intrinsic spirit of the classical disciplines, Tsuji showed great concern for the future of the Mugai Ryu. He wrote: "Among the many who master my teachings only a few master the spirit and essence of swordsmanship. My concern for the future of the Mugai Ryu is that it may be perpetuated in a way that its instrinsic value can benefit those who wish to learn its methods a hundred years from now. An excellent blade and its proper use depend on its user. But those who are not worthy of the Mugai Ryu must not be initiated into its teachings. Selecting the right person for study is a difficult task, much like properly fitting an axle to the hole in a wheel; both depend on sufficient experience. Learning and study alone are not enough. Without hard training and making the techniques [of swordsmanship] your own, that is, until your hands and mind move as one, until you can think automatically and unconsciously, you cannot master swordsmanship. All endeavor in the Mugai Ryu must lead to a high goal—the stage of unification of spirit and technique."

Archery practice

OTHER WEAPONS SYSTEMS The emergence of the classical budo systems did not automatically extinguish the existence of the classical bujutsu systems. All the budo entities, because they dealt with weapons, were initially based on the use of the sword in kendo fashion, yet swordsmanship throughout most of the Edo period remained closely related to its use in combat. Other major weapons of the bujutsu arsenal, such as the *yari* (spear), *nagamaki* (long-bladed, short-shafted halberd), and naginata, did not figure in the initial development of the classical budo forms. These weapons were still considered in the context of their uses in combat as "sharp keys to hell," in spite of the predominantly peaceful nature of the Edo period. Later in the period, however, the mock naginata, patterned after the real weapon, became an important instrument in the development of the budo spirit. The bow and arrow, because its practical use was substantially replaced by firearms, acquired a position of special importance when the classical budo forms were being designed. However, because *kyudo,* the "way of the bow," was not established as a definite budo entity until the twentieth century, it lies beyond the historical scope of this book.

Throughout the Edo period there were flashes of martial ardor that helped halt deterioration of the fighting ability of high-spirited men. After Shogun Iemitsu's death in 1651, for example, the martial strength of the bakufu was so dissipated that it afforded opportunities for some men to show their hatred of the bakufu by recourse to combat. Yui Shosetsu, a commoner inspired by ronin supporters, formed a conspiracy against the bakufu. His accomplice, Marubashi Chuya, a warrior who was expert in the use of the naginata, entered the conspiracy to carry out a personal vendetta against government officials. However, the conspiracy was quickly crushed by the bakufu.

The hardy men who upheld the traditions of the classical warrior provide some of the finest examples of heroic endeavor, and their courageous deeds fill the pages of Japanese annals. Perhaps the spirit of all such men and their expertise with weapons are best illustrated in one of Japan's most treasured epics of martial virtue, the story of the fortyseven ronin. Its details are well recorded, but a summary both of what happened and of the results of the incident are pertinent here.

In 1701 the daimyo of Ako in western Honshu drew his sword under severe provocation and wounded an official of the shogun in Edo. Because drawing a sword in certain official areas was a serious breach of

Archery practice

the law, this daimyo was ordered by the bakufu to commit *seppuku* (ritual suicide by disembowelment). His han was confiscated, and forty-seven of his loyal warriors became masterless ronin. They vowed vengeance on the bakufu official. While under strict surveillance by the bakufu, these men deserted their families, ostensibly leading lives of debauchery in order to veil their greater purpose. When they were no longer carefully watched, they regrouped and entered the official's residence on a cold, snowy night late in 1703 and killed him, thus fulfilling their pledge to avenge the death of their beloved lord.

Behind the action of the forty-seven ronin lies the motive of loyalty to a superior, one of the cardinal virtues of the classical warrior. Their concerted action was *kataki-uchi,* "vendetta," a custom thought honorable and sanctioned by Japanese society. The leader of the ronin was Oishi Kuranosuke, whose mentor was Yamaga Soko (1622–85). Yamaga Soko, one of Japan's "Three Great Ronin," opposed Chu Hsi Neo-Confucianism. His teachings formed much of the basis for what was later called bushido, the "way of the warrior." He infused Kuranosuke, who thought of his function in terms of duty, not reward, with ideas of moral obligation and filial piety. Though Yamaga Soko openly admitted that the function of the warrior in Edo society was largely that of being a civil official, he nevertheless charged the warrior with

Master bowman Suhara Koun, a Rinzai Zen priest at Engaku-ji temple in Kamakura, embodies the spirit of classical kyudo in his calm concentration Shown are various stages of the draw prior to release.

the responsibility for the intellectual and moral guidance of all social classes. He stressed the relationship between the warrior and his superior as something divinely decreed, absolute and inviolable. And so the actions of the forty-seven ronin had their basis in Confucian ideals, specifically the ideal of moral duty. The vendetta required bakufu sanction to make it legal, but for obvious security reasons the forty-seven ronin chose not to notify the bakufu of their intention. For this deliberate breach of law, after their successful act the forty-seven men submitted without demur to the bakufu's order to commit seppuku.

During the interval between the death of their lord and the successful conclusion of their vendetta two years later, the forty-seven ronin engaged in martial disciplines.

Though their purpose was combat, and so was more closely allied in spirit to the bujutsu than to the budo, nevertheless one cannot easily dismiss the spiritual aspects of this training, of which the austerities closely conform to the spirit of the classical budo disciplines. Four major weapons of the classical warrior's arsenal were used by these ronin in their training and in their vendetta: the odachi, the yari, the naginata, and the bow and arrow. This limited selection of weapons is significant. In it is reflected the conservative attitude of the classical warrior, with his contempt for firearms, the "weapons of cowards." The virtue of

Left: Takenouchi Toichiro, headmaster of the Takenouchi Ryu, strikes a kamae *with the* bo, *or hardwood staff.*

honor, which Nitobe Inazo describes as "a vivid consciousness of personal dignity and worth," was strong in all forty-seven loyal men. It made of the indignation that they shared for their cause a righteous wrath. What they were honor-bound to do could only be correctly done by means of the respected instruments of their martial profession. All their martial training was conducted in great secrecy, behind closed doors or under cover of night. The disciplines in which they engaged, though conducted only individually or in small groups, culminated in a concerted course of successful action when they banded together to carry out their vendetta on that fateful night.

The impact of the forty-seven-ronin incident on Japanese society was far-reaching. Sir George Sansom notes in his *History of Japan: 1615–1867*: "There can be no doubt of its influence upon the mind of all classes." The vendetta inspired many warriors and commoners to cultivate the virtue of absolute loyalty. Sansom continues: "It is a curious fact that whereas in the first half of the Yedo period among the recorded cases of kataki-uchi most were the work of bushi, in the second half (except in cases of single combat) farmers and merchants were in a majority. It would thus appear that in the beginning the militant spirit of

Left and above: Maniwa Nen Ryu disciples are shown training with the naginata, *an important weapon in this ryu's curriculum. In both photos the* naginata *is being used against the* bokken.

the bushi had survived from the age of wars, but that with the lapse of time warriors became adjusted to civilian life, while the middle and lower classes gradually came under the influence of the Confucian pattern of behaviour; or perhaps the theatre put ideas into their heads."

This vendetta took place during the rule of the fifth Tokugawa shogun, Tsunayoshi (ruled 1680–1709). Japan at this time was already undergoing a succession of domestic ills, which were worsened by the erratic conduct of the shogun and by the malpractices of his officials in affairs of state. Tsunayoshi was not a warrior, nor was the bakufu any longer a martial organ. Rising taxes, natural catastrophes, an expanding population, food shortages, and the question of how to deal with foreigners combined with the general laxity and corruption of the bakufu officials to produce conditions of unrest throughout the land. These were problems that the bakufu was not equipped to solve. There were rallies and attempts by Tsunayoshi's successors to infuse the country with the classical martial spirit as characterized by frugal living. But such legislation and reform measures as were instituted failed to stem the floodtide of a too rapidly changing society. As the morals and the finances of the bakufu deteriorated, along with those of the warrior

class, the bureaucracy became steadily more impoverished as the eighteenth century progressed.

Japanese society was not in equilibrium. The Tokugawa hegemony, supposedly maintained by the warrior class, was greatly weakened. Among the social forces that threatened the stability of the warrior class in the eighteenth century was the emergence of the commoners in a new and vital role. The mass movement of people from rural areas to the urban centers, attracted by the bright life and the lure of profit, caused the provincial family unit to shrink. Social immobility as instituted by the Tokugawa bakufu became unworkable, and through it all the commoners, though becoming more influential than the warriors, grew restless. This unrest was more a symbol of improved living conditions and the growth of individual self-awareness than it was of economic distress. But social mobility brought together the commoners, with their mutual interests and tastes.

The Edo-period townsmen were culturally dynamic, and they achieved a high degree of literacy and appreciation of the arts. Amid the conditions of improved social freedom that they enjoyed in the large cities, they rapidly became affluent members of society. Their

Left: Kikuchi Taketa, headmaster of the Araki Ryu, uses the kusarigama *to ensnare his opponent's sword. Above: Kikuchi uses the* chigiriki, *a short stick with a weighted chain, to loop the neck of his opponent and hurl him to the ground.*

financial strength allowed them luxuries and led them to seek diversions from the drudgery of making a living. These townsmen were a money-conscious group, and as the great eighteenth-century satirist Ihara Sai-kaku noted, money was "the townsman's pedigree." Many of them found the old classical bujutsu ryu closed to them, but they discovered adequate substitutes in the form of newly founded bujutsu ryu and the emerging classical budo traditions.

It was only natural that the commoners should admire the ideals of the warrior-class elite. They therefore developed their own keen sense of discipline, not too unlike that of the warriors with its emphasis on obligation, honor, and duty. The townsmen developed and maintained elaborate codes of ethics and etiquette, carrying these over into business life. But not all they did was in imitation of the warrior class. There were departures from the strict standards of the warriors, best seen in the townsmen's standards of taste—standards ranging from restrained elegance to flamboyance and garish vulgarity. Their tastes are evident in their choice of daily dress, their decorations, and their flair for artistic expressions, of which the Kabuki theater provides perhaps one of the best examples.

Kabuki is a positive expression of commoner origin that developed in the seventeenth century. The playwright Chikamatsu Monzaemon (1653–1724), who was of samurai rank, gave tremendous impetus to the artistic development of the Kabuki theater, although he wrote his best plays for the puppet theater as the chief playwright for Takemoto Gidayu (1651–1714), a commoner and the major developer of the puppet theater. Greatly influenced by the puppet theater, many of whose plays it adapted, Kabuki grew in the following two centuries to be a most popular medium of entertainment for the townsfolk.

The essence of Kabuki is the exaggeration of form. A deliberate distortion of fact is made in order to set the scene, establish the mood, and produce a pleasant reaction in the viewers. Monzaemon writes of this essence: "Art is something that lies in the slender margin between the real and the unreal. . . . While bearing resemblance to the original it should also have stylization."

The commoners who produced and acted in Kabuki dramas found their chosen medium a superb vehicle for aesthetic displays of action. Many Kabuki scripts were based on warriors' tales or were taken directly from historical incidents involving classical warriors and therefore demanded a considerable use of mock weapons. On stage, toy swords flashed and combats raged, always within Monzaemon's "slender margin." Other mock weapons like the naginata and nagamaki, the *bō* (hardwood staff) and *tessen* (iron hand-fan), countered the sword. The *mitsu-dogu,* the three restraining weapons of the pre-Edo periods (the *sodegarami, tsukubo,* and *sasumata*), were given exaggerated play as symbols of the illustrious past. *Ninja* spies prowled the dark corners of castles on stage, perpetually busy with their esoteric practices. The use of a newer restraining weapon, the *jutte,* a forked iron truncheon, was also glamorized by the actors, who wielded it with unfailing success against obstreperous "samurai" villains. And "experts" in empty-hand combat displayed their fantastic skills to subdue the forces of evil that harassed their loved ones. The play *Chushingura* (The Treasury of Loyal Retainers) popularized the vendetta of the forty-seven ronin, though for fear of reprisals by the bakufu the story was thinly disguised by being set in an earlier period of history.

Other artistic expressions of the Edo period signal the loss of importance of the warrior class and show the rising degree of social mobility, which was rapidly narrowing the distinctions among the various social

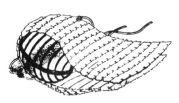

Early men

classes. The poet Matsuo Basho (1644–94), for example, was born into samurai status but renounced its privileges and lived the life of a common man. He became famous as a poet in the *haikai* style, a kind of light-hearted seventeen-syllable verse that often illustrated the more humorous aspects of the merchant class. Haikai is characterized by freedom in expression and is thus diametrically opposed to the serious formality of the classical *waka,* a thirty-one-syllable verse form.

In his haikai Basho showed his disregard for tradition, championing the principle that he suggested to his pupils: "Do not seek to follow in the footsteps of the men of old; seek what they sought." Basho was also famous for his *hokku* (the opening verse of a series of linked verses), which in time became a style in its own right known as *haiku.* Basho's verse has an ever-present sense of warm sympathy and identification with nature. Through the ability to choose contrasting images emphasizing one essential detail, such as a grasshopper resting under the helmet of a dead warrior, Basho expressed universal truths.

The satirical novelist Jippensha Ikku (1766–1831), also a samurai, satirized the warrior class in his *Hizakurige* (Shank's Mare); this comic novel proved to be immensely popular with the townsfolk. Takizawa Bakin (1767–1848), a ronin's son, also became a prolific writer and, under the influence of the ethics of the classical warrior, brought some degree of respect back to that social group.

Yet another art form, the making of woodblock prints known as *ukiyo-e,* "pictures of the floating world," was a fully plebeian endeavor. Ukiyo-e reflected the interests and tastes of the Edo commoners; the artists who produced ukiyo-e, however, depicted subjects that were appreciated by all classes of people. They approached their work in a conscious effort to distort reality but in so doing produced some of the best examples of popular art in Edo times. There is a wide variety of themes in this genre, one of which is *musha-e,* or "warrior pictures." Musha-e depict a wealth of combat lore, but one must be careful to separate the elements of idealization and romanticism in these prints in order to see the truth in them.

Utagawa Toyokuni (1769–1825) established a style of ukiyo-e prints that culminated in the work of great artists like Kunisada (1786–1864), Kuniyoshi (1797–1861), and other talented men whose untiring efforts quickly made musha-e popular with townsfolk. Katsushika Hokusai (1760–1849) and Ando Hiroshige (1797–1858) each developed a distinc-

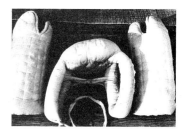

Maniwa Nen Ryu protective gear: helmet and kote

tive style. While giving precedence to themes other than the warrior, these two artists produced a number of fine musha-e; and pupils of these two famous artists also depicted warrior themes.

Among the evidence for rising standards of living in Edo-period society is the social phenomenon known as the *kabukimono* (eccentrics). Although posing as swashbuckling gallants, the kabukimono were actually, as Sansom noted in *A History of Japan: 1615–1867,* "a considerable element of ne'er-do-wells, living on the fringe of respectable society and subsisting upon dubious occupations." Two kinds of kabukimono are germane to both classical bujutsu and classical budo. The first of these is certain Edo warriors who, for lack of anything constructive to do, and feeling the economic pinch, turned to street fighting, robbery, and general knavery. Ronin were involved, but to a lesser extent than the shogun's own special class of warriors, the *hatamoto* (bannermen). The followers of the hatamoto kabukimono were known as *yakko* (underlings). They carried extra-long swords with which to cut down citizens who got in their way. The bakufu was forced to take drastic measures against these, its own men.

Opposed to the hatamoto kabukimono and yakko were the *machi-yakko* (town underlings), bands of young townsmen who claimed to be champions of oppressed commoners. In reality the machi-yakko were no more than rogues themselves, in pursuit of illicit aims. The bakufu rounded them up and executed almost all of them. But the frequent clashes between the two socially different kinds of yakko at least brought some vitality into the use of classical bujutsu systems and served to stimulate the foundation of new ones. Street fights between rival bands of kabukimono also brought an undesirable—to classical budo exponents—suggestion that classical budo disciplines might be of assistance in actual fighting.

The townsmen's generally flamboyant taste, compared with that of the warrior class, was vividly displayed in their art. By the nineteenth century this taste was clearly seen in the classical budo forms, as well. Those budo systems that were either founded by commoners or largely supported by them exhibited the typically flamboyant emotion with which the commoners imbued their other forms of artistic expression. But there was also a sense of refinement in their budo disciplines, achieved by the removal of certain elements of ruggedness that characterized classical bujutsu training.

Stick-fighting training

Training in budo was rarely undertaken in other than specially prepared indoor areas, the dojo. Whereas warriors might occasionally exercise their bujutsu in enclosed areas for the sake of secrecy, it was the accepted custom of the exponents of the classical budo forms to do so. Because of the ideal floor surfaces in the dojo, certain technical peculiarities arose in the budo forms that were absent in the bujutsu. For one, the foothold offered by a smooth, level wooden floor is excellent; that offered by natural terrain is naturally not. Accordingly, the budo techniques evolved in an ideal rather than a realistic environment. The trainee not only could assume very upright postures but could, under these ideal conditions, move without fear of encountering obstacles. As a result, trainees made conscious efforts to achieve beauty in their postures and movements, and a fine artistic impression came to be greatly valued.

The techniques of swordsmanship, in particular, took on combatively inane mannerisms. This is seen in the loss of the sinking of the waist to reinforce cutting actions; the "cut" of the sword was, in kendo, replaced by a "touch" action. And in the *ogiri*, or exaggerated cutting action, used by exponents of iai-do, the swordsman exposes himself (*suki*) to all but the most inexpertly made attack. But the lack of attention paid to either of these considerations is not opposed to the essence of the classical budo, which substitutes spiritual and aesthetic values for combative effect.

Kendo rapidly gained a large following because competition was possible without fear of the participants' being seriously injured. This naturally led to an emphasis on sportlike play, which the townsfolk engaged in as a leisure pastime. But there were those, of course, who regarded swordsmanship purely as a spiritual discipline.

One of the outstanding developments in classical budo training methods was made in the final years of Tokugawa rule. This was the use of the naginata for budo training. By designing a mock weapon that had only a fraction of the weight of the real naginata, naginata techniques underwent vast changes. The mock weapon could be wielded in rapid and exaggerated actions, and the criteria of expertise included artistic appeal. By improving protective equipment it was also possible to match a kendo swordsman against a competitor armed with the mock naginata. This kind of competition proved to be immensely popular with the public, as previously noted.

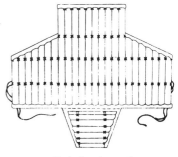

Early kendo *trunk protector,* do

CHAPTER SEVEN

CLASSICAL "WEAPON-LESS" SYSTEMS: FROM JUJUTSU TO JUDO

Ran on embattled armies clad in iron,
and, weaponless himself, made arms
ridiculous.

John Milton

A lack of combative balance is the outstanding characteristic of all budo entities. Combative balance is established and maintained by attaining expertise in a wide range of weapons and familiarity with other martial systems. But the effects of peace in the Edo period eventually eroded this sense of practical realism.

Many ryu founded during this period tended to narrow the scope of their martial curricula. Quite often the exponents of such ryu became specialists in the use of only one weapon, a trend that would, after the fall of the Tokugawa feudal state, become the accepted custom for exponents of budo disciplines. This tendency to overspecialize becomes remarkably clear when one studies the weaponless arts, the so-called "empty-hand" systems.

In a strict sense, no classical bujutsu ryu is entirely based on empty-hand tactics. Furthermore, most classical budo ryu also depend on the use of weapons. The purely empty-hand systems are by and large the product of the Meiji and later eras. In order that this important fact may be seen, and the true nature of empty-hand methods be understood, some background as to the relationship between empty-hand combat and the classical weapons systems is necessary.

The classical warriors had little use for any system of combat that did not use weapons. This was primarily because the opportunity for unarmed combat was rare, being favored by neither custom nor circumstances. The very rationale and mystique that surrounded the classical warrior revolved around his possession of weapons. And the necessities of the time in which he functioned required him to be well armed and trained in the use of deadly weapons. A warrior therefore was never without weapons, even when asleep, and was certainly never without his beloved sword.

Certain technical aspects of classical combat were determined by the use of *katchu* (armor). For the warrior even to entertain the idea of success in combat, in the sense of killing his opponent, he could attack his foe only when armed. The fact that armor was worn influenced the manner in which a warrior would deal with his foe. Mere sparring tactics of a "boxing" nature, which must rely for effect upon the use of the natural parts of the body—hand, fist, foot—in delivering *atemi* (blows directed at anatomically weak points) by striking, punching, or kicking, were hopelessly ineffective and would be likely to result in more injury to the attacker than to the intended victim.

It was quite natural then that close-quarter combat should be characterized by grappling methods. The general word describing these methods of combat was *kumi-uchi,* an expression that suggests the clashing of two combatants at close quarters. These methods of grappling included the liberal use of such atemi as could be delivered through the clever use of major weapons in the initial phases of combat; these were but the prelude to the actual locking with the foe and the use of shorter weapons, such as the *yoroi-doshi,* a heavy-duty dagger that could be plunged into the foe, through his protective armor if necessary.

Among the very oldest of the classical bujutsu traditions the use of the butt ends of the major weapons (odachi, naginata, yari, bo), used for striking in delivering atemi, proved highly effective against an adversary clad in armor. A warrior who was unable skillfully to exploit the spaces between the parts of his foe's armor might simply penetrate the armor itself by breaking through it with the *ishi-zuki,* a special iron device that capped the butt end of his naginata or yari, as his foe concentrated on defending himself from the blade.

A jujutsu tactic

Though the teachings contained in the Tenshin Shoden Katori Shinto Ryu, a fifteenth-century martial tradition, do not mention any systematic kind of grappling to be carried out when wearing armor, there arose within the martial curriculum of this ryu a system called *yawara-ge* ("peacemaker"). Yawara-ge, in the style of the Katori Shinto Ryu, is a kind of grappling combat between persons who may be unarmed with major weapons or who choose not to use their weapons. This system is not absolutely independent of weapons; rather it is a secondary system in which the kodachi, the favorite weapon of Izasa Choiisai Ienao, founder of this ryu, is used. Another of the fifteenth-century ryu, the Muso Jikiden Ryu, also provided warriors with an efficient method for grappling in armor. Choiisai Ienao, while serving as the seventh head-master of that ryu, devised one hundred combat techniques, which he called *yawara-gi* ("meekness"), and integrated them with the Muso Jikiden Ryu teachings. The Muso Jikiden Ryu style of yawara-gi did not absolutely require the exponent to engage his foe in an empty-hand fashion. And when Hasegawa Eshin, famous for his swordsman-ship, became the nineteenth headmaster of the Muso Jikiden Ryu he broadened his experience of yawara-gi and developed one hundred techniques of his own to be used when fighting with a sword.

The Takenouchi Ryu, founded in the first half of the sixteenth cen-tury, featured a kind of grappling with the warrior clad in *kogusoku,* a minimal armor consisting of leggings and gauntlets. This form of grap-pling was called *kogusoku* and was also referred to as *koshi no mawari* (literally, "around the loins") because the exponent wore a short sword and carried a length of cord around his waist. It was not until the time of Takenouchi Kaganosuke, the third headmaster, in the Edo period, in connection with an elaboration of techniques called *torite* (a method of restraining an assailant), that some purely empty-hand methods of com-bat were included in the Takenouchi Ryu.

Araki Mujinsai Mataemon Minamoto no Hidetsuna (1584–1637) as a youth studied swordsmanship under Yagyu Shinkage Ryu masters. As the eleventh headmaster of the Muso Jikiden Ryu, Mujinsai also studied with Kaganosuke and thereafter founded his own style of com-bat, which he first called Araki Ryu torite-kogusoku; later, after add-ing more weapons techniques to this system, he retitled it Moro Budo Araki Ryu kempo, a name that suggests a synthesis of various arts of combat, including empty-hand methods.

A clear-cut shift in emphasis from weapons to empty-hand tactics is revealed in the development of the Yagyu Shingan Ryu. The technical

Swordsman using jujutsu

essence of this ryu is that of combat and stems from the Shinkage Ryu and Yagyu Shinkage Ryu teachings. Ushu Tatewaki founded what would become the Yagyu Shingan Ryu in pre-Edo times. Some generations of headmasters later, in the Edo period, when Takenaga Naoto received official permission from Yagyu Tajima no Kami to name his ryu the Yagyu Shingan Ryu, the martial curriculum was modified. As the Edo period advanced, the empty-hand portion of Naoto's teachings came to dominate the studies of his disciples. But all his empty-hand tactics could be applied in actual combat and could also be used when wearing armor and while armed.

The great kenshi Miyamoto Musashi was also well versed in methods of close-quarter combat. In his youth, as a disciple of the Emmei Ryu just prior to the opening of the Edo period, Musashi studied yawara-ge, which in the Emmei Ryu style was not entirely a weaponless art. It was from this source that Musashi derived his expertise in *kakushi-jutsu,* the art of using small concealed weapons.

The aforementioned ryu, and hundreds more like them, were the product of an age of violent wars. It is clear from a critical examination of the makimono of these ryu that though portions of their martial curricula dealt with empty-hand methods of combat, by and large all such techniques were developed for actual fighting and remained secondary to the use of weapons. The founders and leading exponents of these ryu were all first trained as swordsmen, and in many cases were also expert with other weapons. Even centuries of freedom from war and the tremendous social forces that eventually caused the collapse of the Tokugawa feudal system and resulted in an imperial Meiji-era Japan would do little to weaken or narrow the teachings regarding combat of these, the oldest of the classical bujutsu traditions.

The grappling systems of the classical bujutsu ryu may be conveniently grouped under the generic term *kumi-uchi.* Because domestic peace flourished under Tokugawa rule, there were some men who were determined to create methods of fighting more suited to the social needs of Edo times. From their efforts arose systems of combat generically called *jujutsu,* ostensibly a term that first came into general use during the Edo period and which has since confused laymen.

Watatani Kiyoshi, one of modern Japan's most eminent authorities on the martial culture of his country, declares kumi-uchi to be "the backbone of jujutsu." Watatani notes that some logical classification of

Throwing a swordsman

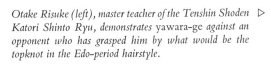

Above: this woodblock print shows one of the forty-eight standard te, or techniques, of sumo wrestling. Note the similarity to a jujutsu hold.

Otake Risuke (left), master teacher of the Tenshin Shoden ▷ *Katori Shinto Ryu, demonstrates* yawara-ge *against an opponent who has grasped him by what would be the topknot in the Edo-period hairstyle.*

Above: this woodblock print by Hokusai shows Edo-period commoners practicing jujutsu.

◁ *Otake Risuke (left) utilizes another yawara-ge technique of the Tenshin Shoden Katori Shinto Ryu, this time breaking the hold of an assailant who has grabbed the front of his kimono.*

techniques must be made and understood before an adequate definition of the word "jujutsu" is possible. Used incorrectly, "jujutsu" embraces far too narrow a variety of systems of combat. The word also gives the mistaken impression that jujutsu is an absolutely weaponless form of combat. The principle of *ju,* "pliancy" or "flexibility," is invoked, and, being misunderstood, gives rise to still further misconceptions regarding the so-called "gentle art," jujutsu.

Watatani draws a firm distinction between the apparel of the classical warriors when 1) fully armored, 2) lightly armored, and 3) completely without armor. The first of these three divisions limits close-quarter combat to that of the *yoroi kumi-uchi* (grappling in armor) type, the second to kogusoku and koshi no mawari, and the third to the kumi-uchi style. In a technical sense the so-called jujutsu systems subsumed all three of these general categories of grappling. But as armor ceased to be worn in the mid-to-late Edo period, it was the kumi-uchi forms that comprised the basis for classical jujutsu. Other influences also helped determine the development of jujutsu in Edo society. From continental Asia the Chinese *ch'uan-fa* ("fist way") systems of sparring, pronounced *kempo* in Japanese, were numbered among the skills of the Japanese who founded jujutsu systems.

Chin Gempin (Chinese, Ch'en Yuan-pin; 1587–1674) was a Chinese-born, naturalized Japanese, a resident of Owari (present Aichi Prefec-

Headmaster Kikuchi Taketa of the Araki Ryu demonstrates torite-kogusoku, *a form of weaponless combat that is a specialty of the ryu. First he gets his victim off balance, then hurls him to the ground and immobilizes him by applying pressure to anatomical weak points.*

ture). Gempin is traditionally believed to have taught three ronin in Edo three tactics (not methods) of ch'uan-fa. The ronin, Fukuno Shichiroemon, Miura Yojiemon, and Isogai Jirozaemon, later founded ryu in which jujutsu was an important part of their teachings. This relationship between Gempin and the ronin has been much overemphasized. The claim that jujutsu is a Chinese art stemming from Chin Gempin's teachings is about as valid as implying that the inventor of the wheel was the developer of the modern automobile. Jujutsu itself is a Japanese product. The historical record clearly shows that a jujutsu-like form of combat was in use even before Gempin came to Japan, and probably before he was born. It also reveals that the three ronin had had considerable experience in other well-established ryu before they founded their own jujutsu styles. No traditional Japanese annals deny that Gempin gave an important impetus to the technical aspects of unarmed combat of the Edo period, specifically jujutsu. But like most that was borrowed from the Asian continent by the Japanese, a native flavor was given to the original form, making of it an adapted rather than an adopted form.

There are several hundred ch'uan-fa styles. All were, in China, basically methods of unarmed combat developed by peasant and merchant groups. It was the southern ch'uan-fa styles that were transferred to Japan; no complete system, however, or thorough study of any ch'uan-fa system appears to have been transmitted to the Japanese. The Japanese referred to these Chinese forms as *hakuda* or *shuhaku*, both terms meaning "to beat by hand." The term "kempo" was also used by the Japanese to describe any and all empty-hand methods of fighting in a sparring manner.

Both the warrior and the commoner engaged in jujutsu during the Edo period, but the latter gave it more notoriety. Jujutsu for the commoners was largely an "empty-hand" method of fighting in the scuffles met with in daily life. As such, jujutsu was most useful to the *nanushi* (managers) of houses of prostitution, such as those in the famed Yoshiwara section of Edo. A warrior who became inebriated and obnoxious would have to be dealt with by the nanushi, whose job it was to get the warrior to quiet down and leave the premises. The rampages of the kabukimono, too, involved a kind of "empty-hand" combat.

In Edo, jujutsu was also popularly spoken of as *yawara,* a term derived by abbreviating the words "yawara-ge" and "yawara-gi." The word "yawara" is a noun created during the Edo period to describe those systems of hand-to-hand combat that are, like jujutsu, based on the principle of *ju,* "pliancy" or "flexibility." Tradition asserts that the term "yawara" was first used to describe the methods of combat designed by Sekiguchi Jushin Hachiroemon Minamoto no Sanechika (1647–1711), the founder of the Sekiguchi Ryu. Jushin based his style of yawara on grappling methods of a kumi-uchi type, specifically *sumo.* He made yawara a secondary system within a system of swordsmanship, batto-jutsu, and also showed that it could by applied when fighting with the spear. Jushin's yawara became popular as separate teachings after his successors narrowed the scope of the ryu to that of the related batto-jutsu. The yawara of the Sekiguchi Ryu retained its essence as a fighting art throughout most of the Edo period.

Oguri Niemon established the Oguri Ryu in 1616. As a disciple of the Yagyu Shinkage Ryu, Niemon was impressed with the need to keep fighting a practical matter even in times of peace. One branch of study in the teachings of the Oguri Ryu was that of *wajutsu,* the "art of softness." Niemon's wajutsu was directly related to systems using weapons, and the actual techniques comprising its repertoire stemmed from the methods of yoroi kumi-uchi. Niemon modified the techniques of grappling designed for use by warriors clad in armor so that they could be applied while wearing normal street clothes.

These portions of a Nagao Ryu hand-scroll illustrate various taijutsu *techniques. Upper left: the butt of the sword hilt is used against an opponent about to draw his blade. Lower left: the bare hand is used to strike the throat of an adversary. Note that both men hold their swords ready for use either drawn or sheathed. Above: a short stick is used to trip an opponent fleeing up a ladder.*

This illustration from a Nagao Ryu hand-scroll on taijutsu *techniques shows the* bankokuchoki *(right), a concealed weapon used to deliver* atemi, *about to be wielded against a swordsman.*

Yet another term used in Edo times to describe jujutsu-like systems was *taijutsu,* a word that literally means "body art." One of the foremost styles of taijutsu centered on the teachings of the Nagao Ryu, founded by Nagao Kemmotsu early in the seventeenth century. Kemmotsu was a swordsman with experience in both the Itto Ryu and the Yagyu Shinkage Ryu. He developed his brand of taijutsu for use in actual combat, keeping foremost the concern for the use of weapons. Exponents of Nagao Ryu taijutsu were well known for their skill in the use of *kakushi,* small concealed weapons, especially the *bankokuchoki* (or *tekkan-zu*), a metal ring grasped in the hand and used to deliver atemi. The Nagao Ryu was popular among commoners throughout the Edo period, and its martial scope was gradually narrowed through increasing emphasis on empty-hand methods.

The waning years of the period saw most of the oldest, pre-Edo classical bujutsu ryu still hidden from commoners. But the fragmentation of some of these ryu into a number of different styles provided commoners with a chance to obtain information regarding martial matters that had heretofore been unavailable. On the other hand, the increasing interest of commoners in the classical budo disciplines gave an impetus to enterprising people to seek limited knowledge of the classical bujutsu systems, especially "empty-hand" combat methods. Given the strict

Headmaster Takenouchi Toichiro of the Takenouchi Ryu demonstrates this ryu's use of short weapons in kogusoku *grappling. Here he has subdued an opponent and threatens him with the* kodachi.

laws of the Tokugawa bakufu, which forbade commoners to carry weapons, it was quite natural that they should have favored methods of fighting that did not call for weapons.

Jujutsu-like systems thus developed along two mainstreams. In their original forms, as determined by the oldest, pre-Edo classical bujutsu ryu of the warrior class, jujutsu-like systems (yawara-ge, yawara-gi, kogusoku, koshi no mawari, torite, yawara, wajutsu, taijutsu) were but secondary systems related to the use of weapons, and were designed wholly for use in battlefield combat. Other bujutsu ryu of the warriors, created in the Edo period and featuring jujutsu-like techniques, were designed for combat in civil life for the enforcement of law and order in a peaceful society.

On the other hand, bujutsu ryu created by commoners in the Edo period, and those ryu that were supported mainly by commoners, had their scope narrowed to stress only methods of empty-hand combat. This narrowing of the martial curriculum was unavoidable, even if not intentional. For though these bujutsu ryu may originally have dealt essentially with matters of combat, the general lack of professional martial experience among commoners, their lack of expertise with a wide range of weapons, and their lack of proficiency in martial studies did not allow them to create systems that were combatively sound.

This overspecialization in empty-hand jujutsu, as practiced by commoners, had yet another effect on the manner in which the systems were designed. It caused the gradual degeneration of their jujutsu into an aesthetic discipline that had much in common with the noncombative spirit of the classical budo forms. A brief discussion of some of the bujutsu ryu that eventually developed an aesthetic kind of jujutsu makes this clear.

The Kito Ryu is an outstanding example of how a method that is essentially designed for use in combat can be channeled so as to create a purely aesthetic form of endeavor; for in the Meiji era the Kito Ryu, in its aesthetic form, became one of the bases for the development of the modern cognate budo form called Kodokan Judo, itself a weakened form of combat based on empty-hand methods. Ibaragi Sensai, a warrior of low status, was trained as a swordsman in the Yagyu Shinkage Ryu style. He founded the Kito Ryu just prior to the opening of the Edo period. The curriculum of the Kito Ryu, in Sensai's time, was fully devoted to battlefield situations, for it embraced such studies as kenjutsu, iai-jutsu, *bojutsu* (staff fighting), yoroi kumi-uchi, and a number of techniques using minor weapons, among them the *kusarigama,* a composite weapon consisting of a sickle and weighted chain. But later headmasters severely modified Sensai's original teachings and changed the technical direction of the ryu so that it became divorced from studies of actual battlefield fighting.

A jujutsu hand hold

This process began subtly enough. Sensai's successors were greatly influenced by the teachings of the Teishin Ryu and others in which an emphasis on wajutsu prevailed over the methods of iai-jutsu and kogusoku, which were also in its curriculum. The third headmaster of the Kito Ryu, Terada Heizaemon, a samurai of low rank, was the founder of the Teishin Ryu. He had earlier studied with the second headmaster of the Kito Ryu, Fukuno Shichiroemon. The latter had also founded his own style of combat, which he embodied in the teachings of his Fukuno Ryu; prominent in the teachings of this ryu were unarmed techniques of a kempo nature, which Shichiroemon is thought to have learned from Chin Gempin. The fifth headmaster of the Kito Ryu was Terada Kan'emon, also a samurai of low status and the grandson of Heizaemon. Kan'emon learned his basic skills from studies under the supervision of his grandfather, but he displayed considerable individuality upon his assumption of authority as the headmaster of the Kito Ryu.

From this time on, the Kito Ryu teachings not only were narrowed in scope but were aesthetically oriented, bearing little resemblance to those that had comprised the original Kito Ryu. Kan'emon placed strong emphasis on the development of form in the execution of techniques and was less concerned with physical results than he should have been when dealing with any realistic art of combat. He regarded his empty-hand methods, modifications of kumi-uchi techniques, as the central study in his interpretation of the Kito Ryu. Kan'emon declared his empty-hand techniques to be *ran,* "freedom," and encouraged his disciples to *ran o toru,* that is, to "take freedom" in the execution of their techniques, insisting that they move about freely and make changes when they saw fit. Kan'emon was emphatic in declaring that "ran" was something quite distinct from jujutsu.

Kan'emon was left with a certain feeling of dissatisfaction with regard to empty-hand techniques when he retired from his post as headmaster of the Kito Ryu. He thereupon founded an eclectic organization of his own, the Jikishin Ryu. The sole study of this ryu was empty-hand techniques. Because he stressed the mental aspect of training, Kan'emon felt that neither the term "ran" nor the term "jujutsu" properly described his teachings. He chose the word "judo" to describe his system. This term is composed of two ideograms: *ju,* which refers to the principle of pliancy or flexibility, and *dō,* which describes the philosophical concept of *michi,* or way. Kan'emon's is the first known use of the word "judo." The Jikishin Ryu thus became the first classical budo ryu to establish the use of purely empty-hand techniques as a spiritual discipline. In so doing, it approached empty-hand techniques in a revolutionary way.

Iso Mataemon (d. 1862) began his martial studies at the age of fifteen. As a dedicated disciple of both the Yoshin Ryu and the Shin no Shinto Ryu, both of which included very little study for martial ends, Mataemon gained mastery of empty-hand skills. He founded the Tenjin Shin'-yo Ryu in the first half of the nineteenth century in order to perpetuate his teachings, which emphasized an empty-hand approach to jujutsu. It was personal experience, gained some years prior to the foundation of his ryu, that made Mataemon conduct intensive research on atemi. He had confronted, almost single-handed, a large number of rogues, and routed them by means of tactics that involved using hands, fists, elbows, and feet. Atemi became the specialty of the exponents of the Tenjin Shin'yo Ryu, and the effectiveness of Mataemon's skill

Judo

Swordsman subduing man with staff

attracted a great number of aspirants, for the most part commoners, to his dojo.

Though Mataemon's jujutsu depended on an empty-hand approach to combat, he never lost sight of the need for realism in training. Being a samurai, though of a very low status, he was fully aware of the necessity of dealing with dangerous weapons. Mataemon declared that skill in jujutsu was to be achieved through devotion to the method of kata. He said that the nature of kata was *ikemono,* the representation of a "living thing" or situation in combat.

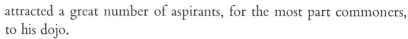

During a *mondo,* a Zen method of teaching by question and answer that was adopted by masters of the bujutsu and budo forms, when asked by one of his disciples what was the best way to face an enemy, Mataemon said: "Pay attention to the *kiki-ude* [naturally used arm], but though most people are right-handed, do not neglect the fact that many can use their left arms almost equally as well. Regard the eyes of the enemy as the windows of his mind, and learn to see what he intends to do, before he actually does it, by looking into his eyes. If the foe does not move about much, remain completely defensive. When you make your attack, *ki o mitasu* [fill yourself with ki], and approach the moment with the idea in mind that this is a fight to the finish.

Jujutsu

"Do not hate your enemy, for hate leads to rash actions, a waste of precious energy, and causes *suki* [gaps in defense]. Keep a tranquil mind, relax your muscles, and keep alert; ki-ai with your mouth closed so as not to let ki dissipate or escape entirely. When you lift with your right hand, as in preparation for making a throw, guard your right leg; in throwing by means of your right leg, take care lest the foe attack your left leg. Move foward against your enemy, but push or pull him off his midline on a diagonal to unbalance him."

Mataemon's concern for realism in combat is apparent. Later headmasters, however, lacked either Mataemon's outlook or the skill with which to maintain the practical realism that its founder had instilled in the Tenjin Shin'yo Ryu. In the Meiji and later eras the teachings of this ryu degenerated into an aesthetic approach using empty-hand tactics in abstract situations.

A jujutsu *arm hold*

In the Edo period more than seven hundred different classical ryu called for the use of jujutsu-like movements in their curricula. There is little evidence to show that more than a minority of these ryu required for their jujutsu methods an essentially weaponless approach. The trend to become less realistic, in regard to combat, would come into focus in the Meiji era and would serve as the basis for an extended development of empty-hand and other categories of study for the purpose of aesthetic and quasi-martial discipline. Inasmuch as the emphasis on realism in combat dominated the teachings of most ryu, it is also quite clear that the principle of ju, which underlies the operation of many of these "empty-hand" methods, likewise contained a practical bias.

The principle of ju underlies all classical bujutsu methods and was adopted by the developers of the budo disciplines. Acting according to the principle of ju the classical warrior could intercept and momentarily control his enemy's blade when attacked, then, in a flash, could counterattack with a force powerful enough to cleave armor and kill the foe. The same principle of ju permitted an unarmed exponent to unbalance and hurl his foe to the ground.

Ju

Terms like "jujutsu" and "yawara" made the principle of ju the all-pervading one in methods catalogued under these terms. That principle was rooted in the concept of pliancy or flexibility, as understood in both a mental and a physical context. To apply the principle of ju, the exponent had to be both mentally and physically capable of adapting himself to whatever situation his adversary might impose on him.

These are two aspects of the principle of ju that are in constant operation, both interchangeable and inseparable. One aspect is that of "yielding," and is manifest in the exponent's actions that accept the enemy's force of attack, rather than oppose him by meeting his force directly with an equal or greater force, when it is advantageous to do so. It is economical in terms of energy to accept the foe's force by intercepting and warding it off without directly opposing it; but the tactic by which the force of the foe is dissipated may be as forcefully made as was the foe's original action.

The principle of ju is incomplete at this point because yielding is essentially only a neutralization of the enemy's force. While giving way to the enemy's force of attack there must instantly be applied an action that takes advantage of the enemy, now occupied with his attack, in the form of a counterattack. This second aspect of the principle of ju makes allowance for situations in which yielding is impossible because it would lead to disaster. In such cases "resistance" is justified. But such opposition to the enemy's actions is only momentary and is quickly followed by an action based on the first aspect of ju, that of yielding. There is no

A jujutsu hold

reason to insist that, in following the principle of ju, an enemy's attack be first met by yielding to it. It is the constant interplay of yielding and resisting that is the principle of ju and that makes Japanese methods of combat the dynamic systems they are.

There were certain jujutsu systems in which less stress was laid on the aspect of yielding than was usual in other ryu. Notable are the teachings of Ichikawa Mondaiyu, a warrior who taught reliance on brute strength as the best way to overcome a foe. Mondaiyu referred to his style of combat as *kowami,* which implies "tough physical exercise." Other systems, such as that of the Muteki Ryu, sought a balance between yielding and resisting. Jujutsu in the style of this ryu was known as *yawara-riki,* or "pliancy in strength."

Even late in the Edo period, when the development of aesthetic disciplines based on martial concepts was growing in popularity, the practical essence of ju had not yet been obscured, let alone forgotten. Iso Mataemon of the Tenjin Shin'yo Ryu comments: "The use of power [physical strength] in jujutsu is greatly necessary. But it is only when such power is not used in excess that it stands the test of the principle of ju. Another aspect of the use of power must be borne in mind, too. From the early stages of a trainee's development in jujutsu he must always be careful to avoid reliance on physical strength, for such is an obstacle in the way of his progress toward the gaining of skill in technique. After the trainee has developed a creditable technique, however, then the use of power is acceptable and, in fact, absolutely necessary to his effectiveness in dealing with an adversary. Jujutsu is 'pliant' and 'flexible' in this way."

Attacking from behind in jujutsu *fashion*

In the Meiji era and later there was a rise in the spirit of ultranationalism. Both the classical bujutsu and classical budo disciplines were harnessed to the task of developing a high degree of martial ardor in the Japanese people. This process was justified by scholars deeply learned in Chinese philosophy, whose embellishments to and distortions of philosophical concepts modified the purposes for which the classical disciplines had been intended. In addition, the creation and application of the modern cognate bujutsu and budo forms assisted the growth of the spirit of ultranationalism, and these latter entities became the basis of a national form of physical culture utilized for the purposes of militarism. These subjects, however, lie outside the framework of this book.

CHAPTER EIGHT

THE CLASSICAL BUDO TODAY

Their exercises are
battles without
bloodshed.
Josephus Flavius

It is immensely worthwhile for any person in modern society to engage
in the study of a classical budo of his choice because classical budo
teaches calmness and emotional stability, two qualities that benefit all
men equally. But there are problems to be surmounted before the
modern person can make such a study.

Most of what has already been written about classical martial disciplines in modern society, such as the information in the first volume of
this series, *Classical Bujutsu,* is applicable to the classical budo; but some
additional comments are pertinent. Classical budo lies at the hearth of
Japanese feudal-age traditions. It is guarded by its exponents with the
strength of their respect for those traditions. Because classical budo hides
from modern society by choice, the location of a master teacher becomes no easy matter. In addition, once accepted by a master for study,
a process which in itself may severely try the candidate's determination,
there is yet another problem to be solved. This is one that concerns the
candidate's right frame of mind—one that will allow him to pursue the
study of a classical discipline. It is vitally important for him to learn to
have a great deal of generosity, so as to become tolerant enough to respect traditional ideas and thought. The spirit of tolerance, in fact, is the
most significant factor making Japan a museum of classical disciplines,
one of which the candidate wishes to study. It is therefore absolutely
essential to his appreciation of the classical budo for him to try to understand its basic spirit and not to overvalue its byproduct, technical skill.

The luxurious, lazily convenient life of the average Westerner is the very antithesis of the spirit of classical budo. When the trainee realizes this, and makes what amounts to a reversion to a more primitive way of life, he will make good progress. The trainee must also become absorbed in *furyu*, that is, the manners, customs, and beliefs handed down from past Japanese generations; this helps him develop an aesthetic sense of values which, in turn, prepares his mind for the process of spiritualization. Through the confrontation of his self with nature, using the medium of the prescribed disciplines, he travels over the "way."

It is true that the classical budo were created by men who sought to escape from the social trammels of their feudal society. But the modern exponent of the classical disciplines should not expect to enter into and remain in a suprasocial world through his practice of these disciplines. A peculiarity of the classical dō forms is that they lead the trainee to seek freedom in compliance with the human nexus. He has volunteered (and let us not forget this essential motivation) to travel over the "way," well aware that the significance of life lies in the doing, the process, rather than the deed, the final completion. Only in this state of mind can he hope to rise above his petty self and achieve self-realization.

Some people make the error of criticizing the classical budo itself rather than the shortcomings of some of its professed followers, such as trainees who engage in the disciplines without the proper spirit. Shallow people will find the shallow wherever they go, but the essence of the classical budo has unsounded depths. An old Japanese saying states that "only the strongest fish dare swim in deep water," and so it is with the exponent who makes classical budo a lifelong study. These disciplines become a way of life for him, not simply a way for part of life; they become a way of feeling, doing, and being. The exponent must continuously bring something from deep inside himself to his study, always expecting to put more into that study than he will ever take out.

Classical budo is not a trifling matter begun for fun or whim. And it is not to be engaged in for personal pleasure or social amusement. Those who would seek to use the dojo for refined exhibitionism, peacock pride, social climbing, chitchat, or gossip have failed to grasp the fact that the profundity of the classical budo exceeds love of self. Classical budo is the endorsement of traditional Japanese values, the objective character of which is cultural. A non-Japanese who objects to being "Japanized" is advised to refrain from entering on a study of classical

Swordsman with fukuro shinai

budo, for its disciplines operate in a very pronouncedly Japanese manner. Should the classical budo be changed to conform to the liking of non-Japanese societies, it would no longer be Japanese classical budo.

The spirit of self-perfection rather than self-protection is supreme in the classical budo. These disciplines are not intended to serve as systems of self-defense, witness the fact that the most skillful experts of these disciplines are famed more for their perfection of character than for their fighting abilities. If it is a system of self-defense that is desired the reader is advised to seek his study within either the classical bujutsu or the modern cognate disciplines developed for that purpose.

Any trainee who expects to find a sport application in his study of classical budo must also be advised to direct himself to the modern cognate disciplines designed for that purpose. It is patent that no sport can ever be a true classical dō form; no classical dō form can ever house a sport entity. The primary purpose of a sport form is the establishment of better records or championships, as well as the development of individual stars or champions. Within that narrow application of the human spirit most people can reach only a gyo level of achievement. When a sport form is carried out with extremely unusual dedication to training disciplines it may approximate the shugyo level. Sport expression carried to the apex of skill for records or championships achieves its ultimate potential, the level of jutsu. There sport is forever doomed to rest. The heights of the dō level are beyond its reach. To become a classical dō a sport entity must drop all notions of competition and record-breaking, of immediate results for championships, of garnering group prestige, and concentrate upon the individual's self-perfection as the end point of training.

Though this present volume cannot hope to answer all the reader's questions about classical budo, it may serve to whet his appetite for more knowledge about these fascinating disciplines. To aid the reader in his search for that knowledge the name and address of a Japanese national organization that has cognizance over all classical ryu in Japan are listed below. All queries concerning the classical disciplines should be addressed to this organization:

Furyu

Kobudo Shinkokai
3, Kojimachi 6-chome
Chiyoda-ku, Tokyo 102

Glossary-Index

Note: Page numbers in italics indicate illustrations.

The "weathermark" identifies this book as a production of Weatherhill, publishers of fine books on Asia and the Pacific. Book design and typography by Ronald V. Bell. Cover design by D. S. Noble. The text is set in Bembo, with Optima for display.